UNITED NATIONS CONFERENCE ON TRADE AND DEVELOPMENT

UNCTAD

D1823343

2017

HANDBOOK OF
STATISTICS

UNITED NATIONS
New York and Geneva, 2017

The world by development status

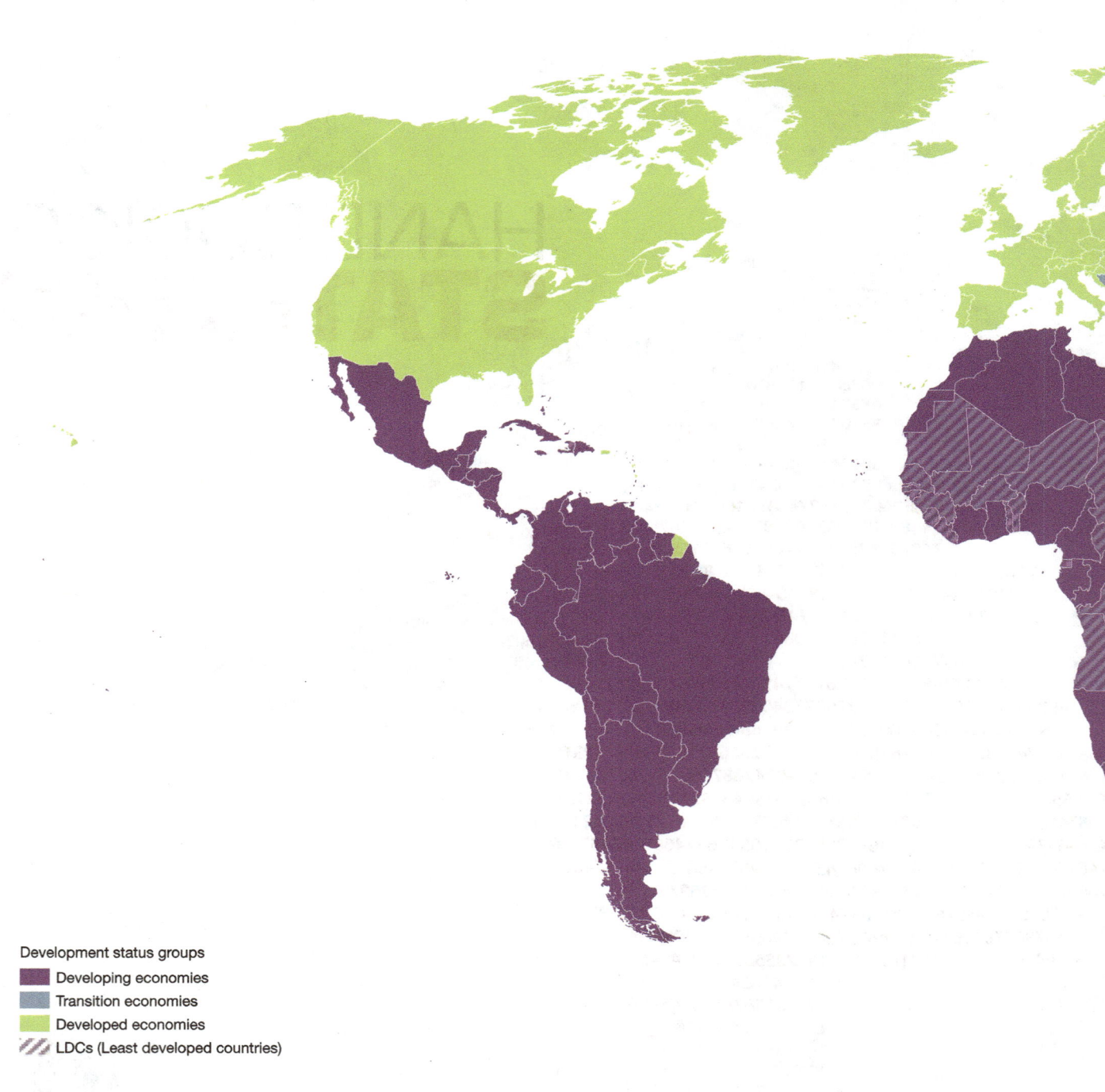

Development status groups
- Developing economies
- Transition economies
- Developed economies
- LDCs (Least developed countries)

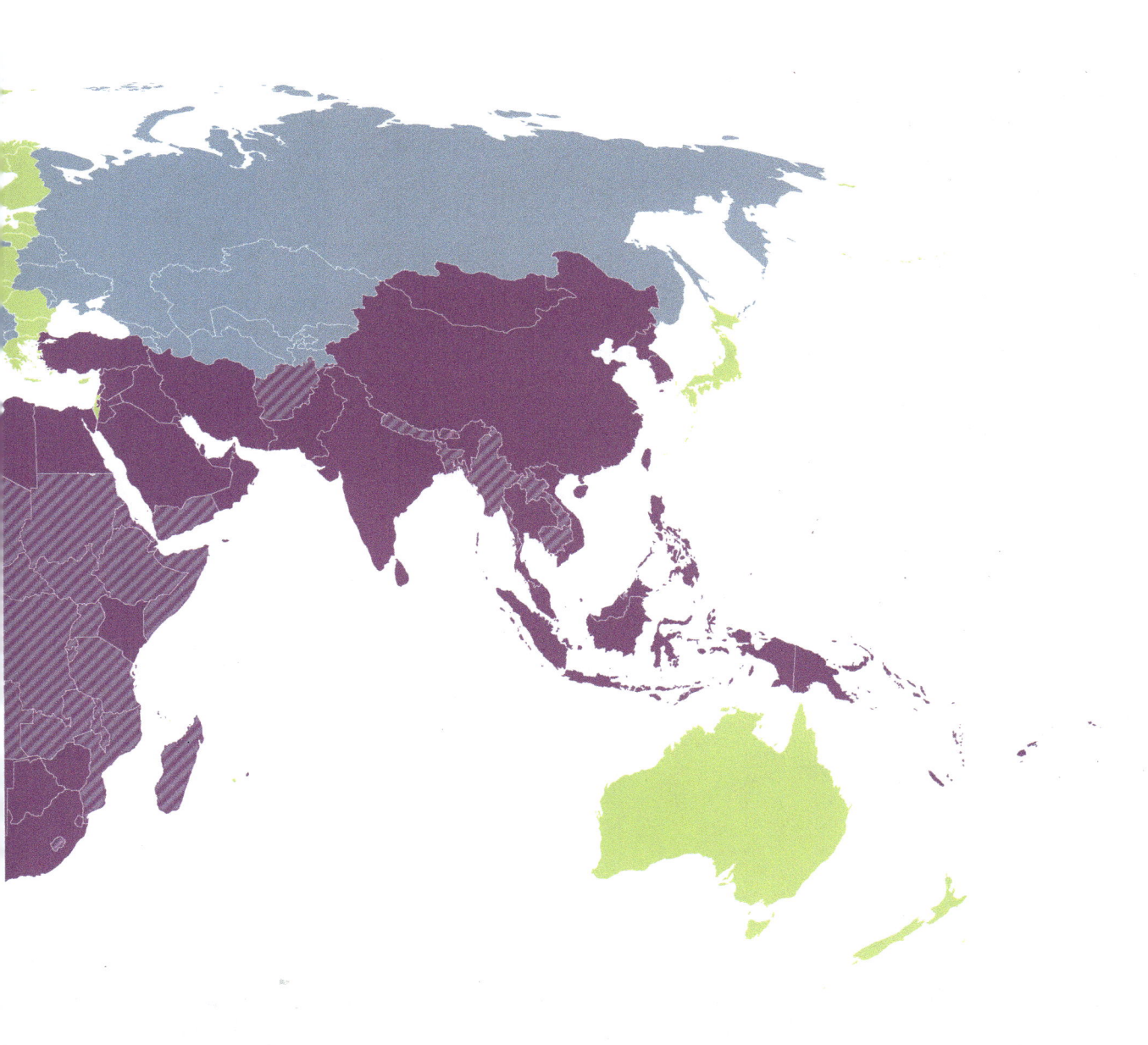

Requests to reproduce excerpts or to photocopy should be addressed to the Copyright Clearance Center at copyright.com.

All other queries on rights and licences, including subsidiary rights, should be addressed to:

United Nations Publications
300 East 42nd Street
New York, New York 10017
United States of America
Email: publications@un.org

Website: shop.un.org

The designations employed and the presentation of material on any map in this work do not imply the expression of any opinion whatsoever on the part of the United Nations concerning the legal status of any country, territory, city or area or of its authorities, or concerning the delimitation of its frontiers or boundaries.

United Nations publication issued by the United Nations Conference on Trade and Development.

TD/STAT. 42
ISBN: 978-92-1-112916-8
eISBN: 978-92-1-362276-6
Print ISSN: 1992-8408
Online ISSN: 2225-3270
Sales No.: E.17.II.D.7

Notes

The tables in this handbook represent extractions from or analytical summaries of the datasets contained in the UNCTADstat data portal, available at:

http://unctadstat.unctad.org/

UNCTADstat is continuously updated and enhanced, thus providing users with the latest available data. Consequently, the figures from this handbook, which presents statistics at one point in time, may not always correspond to the figures in UNCTADstat.

Basic information on concepts, definitions and calculation methods of the presented data is provided in the boxes titled "Concepts and definitions" in each section and in annex 6.3 of this handbook. Detailed information on the sources and methods used for the production of the UNCTADstat data can be found in the documentation attached to the respective UNCTADstat dataset (UNCTAD, 2017a).

Where the designation "economy" appears, it refers to a country, a territory or an area. The assignment of economies to specific groups is done for statistical convenience and does not imply any assumption regarding the political or other affiliation of these economies by the United Nations. Likewise, the designations "developing", "transition" and "developed" are intended for statistical convenience and do not necessarily express a judgement about the stage reached by a particular economy in the development process.

Unless otherwise specified, the values of groups of economies represent the sums of the values of the individual economies included in the group. Calculation of these aggregates may take into account data estimated by the UNCTAD secretariat that are not necessarily reported separately. In cases in which an insufficient number of data points are available within a group of economies, no aggregation is undertaken and the symbol (-) is assigned.

Due to rounding, values do not necessarily add up exactly to their corresponding totals.

United States dollars (US$) are expressed in current United States dollars of the year to which they refer, unless otherwise specified.

Due to space constraints, the names of the following countries may appear in abbreviated form: the Plurinational State of Bolivia, the Democratic People's Republic of Korea, the Democratic Republic of the Congo, the Islamic Republic of Iran, Lao People's Democratic Republic, the Federated States of Micronesia, the former Yugoslav Republic of Macedonia, the United Kingdom of Great Britain and Northern Ireland, and the Bolivarian Republic of Venezuela.

The *UNCTAD Handbook of Statistics 2017* is available as a printed copy or in PDF format from the UNCTAD website, at http://unctad.org/en/Pages/Publications/Handbook-of-Statistics.aspx.

Handbook
of Statistics

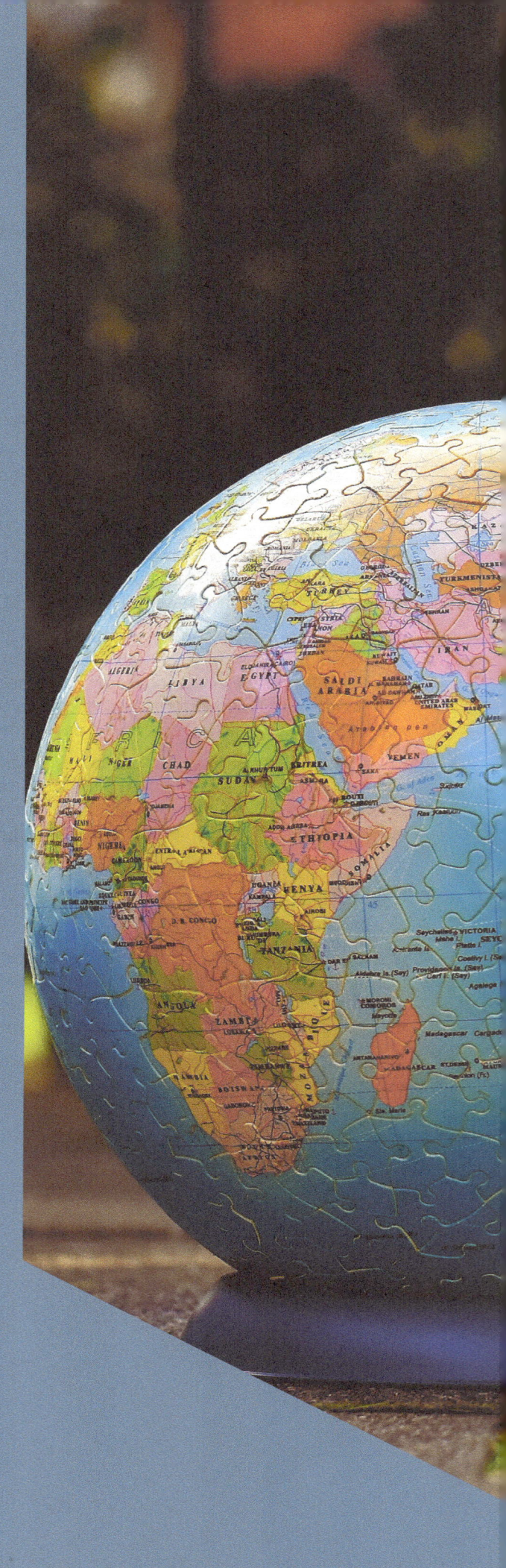

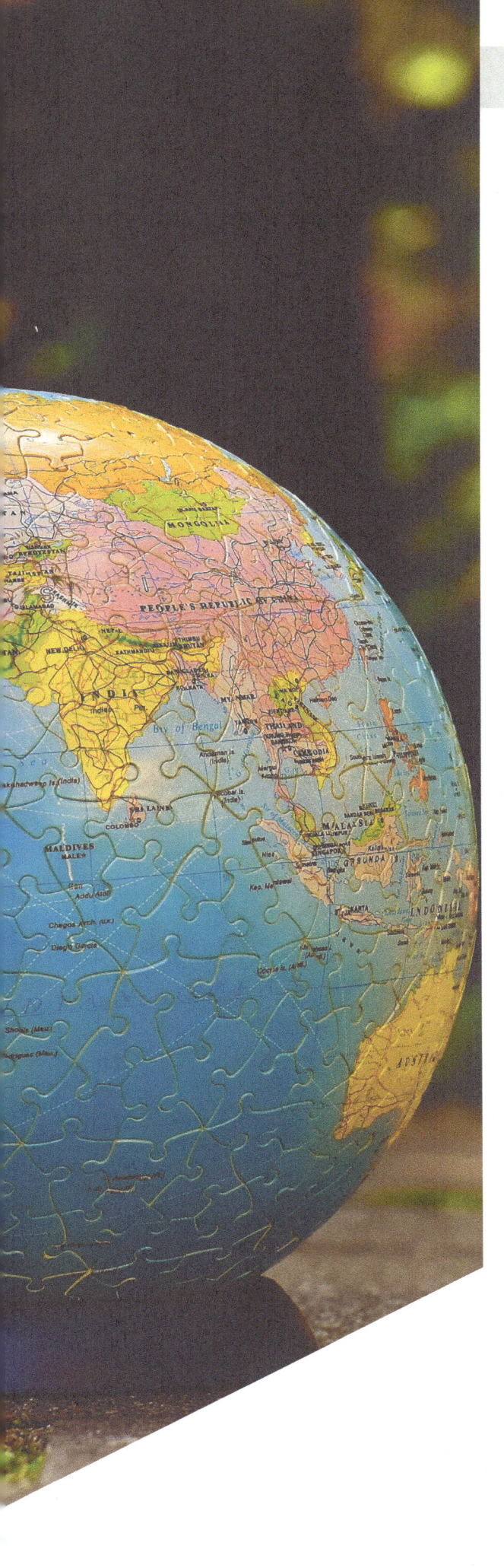

TABLE OF **CONTENT**

List of maps and figures

List of tables

Introduction

The *UNCTAD Handbook of Statistics* was first launched in 1967. Over the past 50 years, the series has evolved to incorporate new statistics and ensure that readers have access to the best possible information available. The 2017 edition of the UNCTAD Handbook of Statistics continues in this tradition of excellence and innovation. On the fiftieth anniversary of the first edition of the UNCTAD Handbook of Statistics, UNCTAD is proud to launch this new, updated version. A new presentation style is designed to integrate the detailed and lengthy statistical time series available from the UNCTADstat data centre with summary tables, state-of-the-art charts, maps and modern infographics.

As with previous editions, the *UNCTAD Handbook of Statistics 2017* continues to provide a wide range of statistics and indicators relevant to the analysis of international trade, investment and development. Reflecting the importance of maritime statistics, this edition of the *Handbook* also includes a new chapter dedicated to this critical topic. Reliable statistical information is indispensable for formulating sound policies and recommendations that may commit countries for many years as they strive to integrate into the world economy and improve the living standards of their citizens. Whether for research, consultation or technical cooperation, UNCTAD needs reliable and internationally comparable trade, financial and macroeconomic data, covering several decades and for as many countries as possible. The *Handbook* and the databases available through UNCTADstat provide those data.

The *UNCTAD Handbook of Statistics* provides users – policymakers, research specialists, academics, officials from national Governments, representatives of international organizations, journalists, executive managers and members of non-governmental organizations – with access to internationally comparable sets of data, in addition to facilitating the work of the UNCTAD secretariat. The Handbook also presents a summary overview of the statistical time series available from UNCTADstat.

Abbreviations and Symbols

Abbreviations

BRICS	Brazil, Russia, India, China and South Africa
CIF	cost, insurance and freight
Dem. Rep.	Democratic Republic
dwt	dead-weight tons
EBOPS	Extended Balance of Payments Services
FDI	Foreign direct investment
FOB	free on board
GDP	gross domestic product
gt	gross tons
G20	Group of Twenty
HIPCs	heavily indebted poor countries
IMF	International Monetary Fund
ISIC	International Standard Industrial Classification of All Economic Activities
LDCs	least developed countries
LLDCs	landlocked developing countries
LSBCI	liner shipping bilateral connectivity index
LSCI	liner shipping connectivity index
Rep.	Republic
SAR	Special Administrative Region
SIDS	small island developing States
SITC	Standard International Trade Classification
TEU	twenty-foot equivalent unit
TFYR	the former Yugoslav Republic
UN-OHRLLS	United Nations Office of the High Representative for the Least Developed Countries, Landlocked Developing Countries and the Small Island Developing States
US$	United States dollars

Symbols

0   Zero means that the amount is nil or negligible.

_   The symbol underscore indicates that the item is not applicable.

..   Two dots indicate that the data are not available or are not separately reported.

-           The use of a hyphen on data area means that data is estimated and included in the aggregations but not published.

A hyphen between years (e.g. 1985 -1990) signifies the full period involved, including the initial and final years.

(e)   Estimated data

(u)   Preliminary estimate

International Merchandise Trade

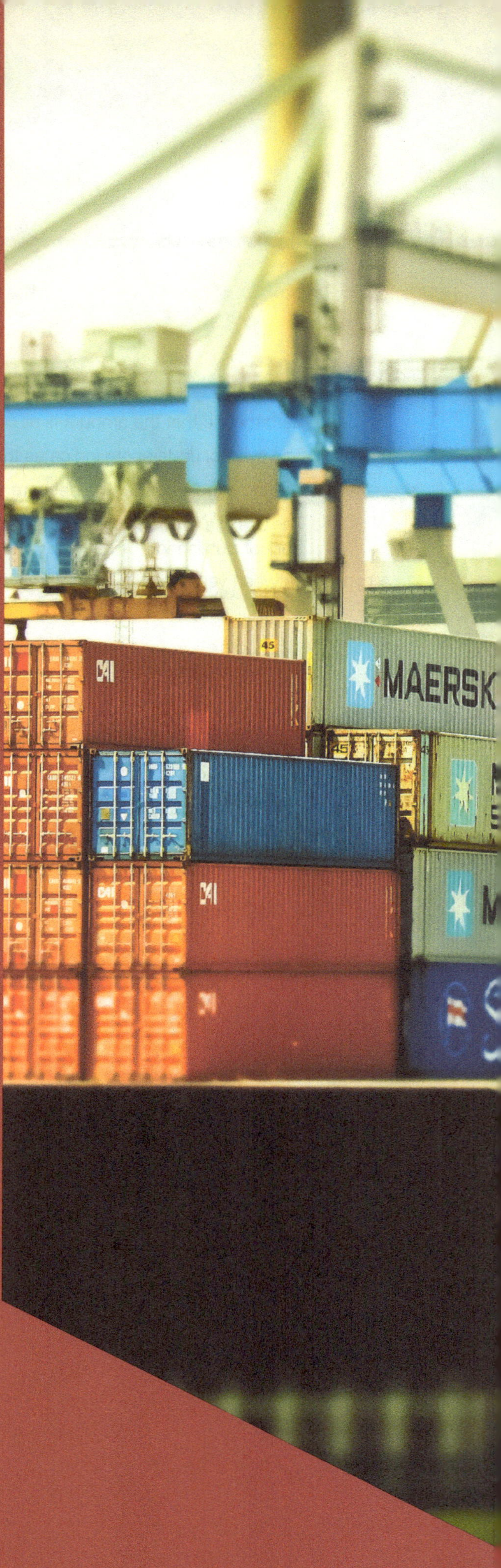

KEY FIGURES **2016**

Growth of world merchandise trade

-3.0%

Value of world merchandise exports

US$16.0 trillion

Share of South-South trade in global trade

27%

LDCs' trade deficit in relation to imports

33%

1.1 Total merchandise trade

Map 1.1 | **Total merchandise exports, 2016**

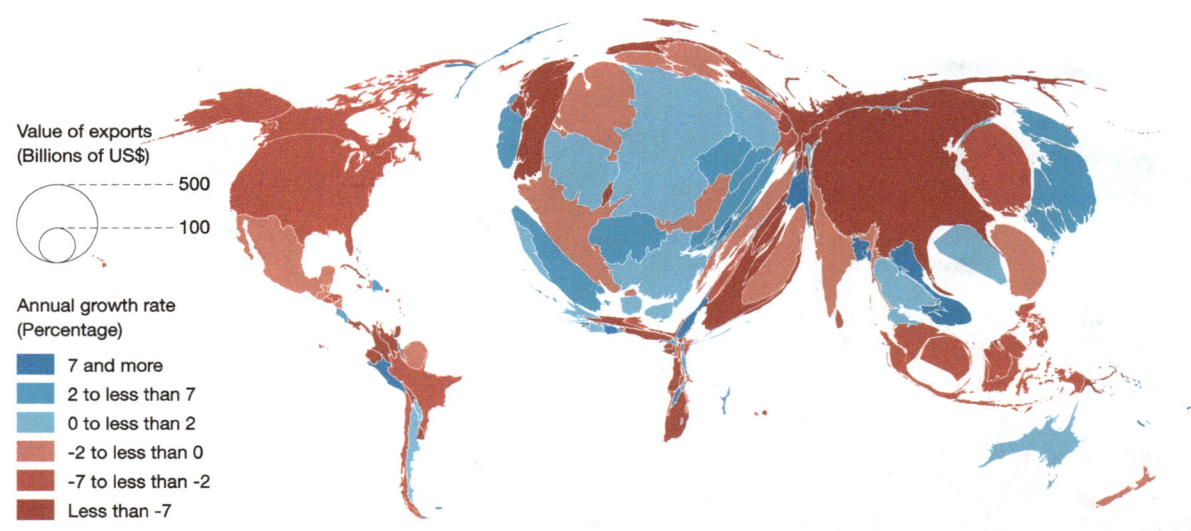

Value of exports
(Billions of US$)

500

100

Annual growth rate
(Percentage)

- 7 and more
- 2 to less than 7
- 0 to less than 2
- -2 to less than 0
- -7 to less than -2
- Less than -7

Concepts and definitions

The figures on international merchandise trade in this chapter measure the value of goods which add or subtract from the stock of material resources of an economy by entering or leaving its territory (United Nations, 2011). This definition is slightly different from the definition of trade in goods in the balance-of-payments framework (see chapter 3.2).

The value of exports is mostly recorded as the free-on-board (FOB) value, whereas the value of imports includes cost (for clearance), insurance and freight (CIF).

The trade balance is calculated as the difference between the values of exports and imports.

Global trends and patterns

In 2016, world merchandise trade valued in United States dollars decreased for the second year in a row. Global exports of US$16.0 trillion were recorded, that is, US$502 billion (3 per cent) less than in 2015. World exports thus fell below 2008 levels (US$16.1 trillion), the year of the outbreak of the global financial crisis.

China (US$2.1 trillion), the United States of America (US$1.5 trillion) and Germany (US$1.3 trillion) were the world's largest exporting economies. In general, exports were dominated by developed economies. Exports of many developing economies in Africa and America were low relative to their size.

In spite of the global decline in trade, many large exporters in Europe as well as in Eastern and South-Eastern Asia increased their sales of goods on the world market in 2016.

Figure 1.1.1 | **World merchandise exports**
(Trillions of United States dollars)

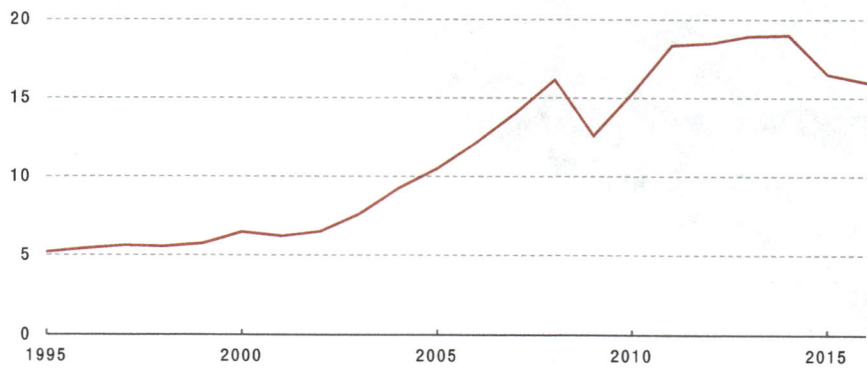

Different exposure to the decline in trade

Transition economies recorded a particularly steep decrease (-15 per cent) in merchandise exports. The fact that imports decreased much less (-1 per cent) had a negative effect on their aggregate trade balance. Developing economies in Africa were also relatively strongly affected by the decline in trade, both for exports (-11 per cent) and imports (-11 per cent). Developing economies in America experienced a sizeable drop (-9 per cent) in their imports and a smaller decrease in exports (-4%).

Figure 1.1.2 | **Merchandise trade annual growth rates, 2016**
(Percentage)

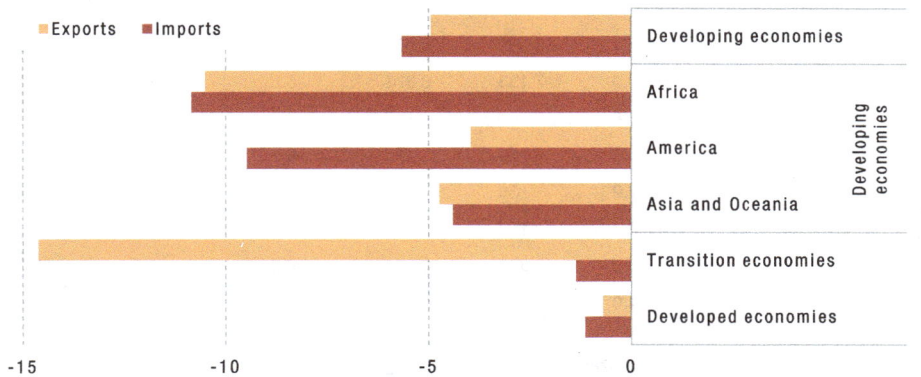

Trade imbalances decreasing

In 2016, as in the past, developing and transition economies recorded merchandise trade surpluses and developed economies a merchandise trade deficit. The surpluses of developing and transition economies were lower than was the case three years earlier. The surplus for developing economies totaled US$397 billion, accounting for 6 per cent of their merchandise imports. Excluding China, the result would be a deficit equivalent to 2 per cent. For least developed countries (LDCs), the deficit amounted to 33 per cent of imports.

Figure 1.1.3 | **Merchandise trade balance***
(Billions of United States dollars)

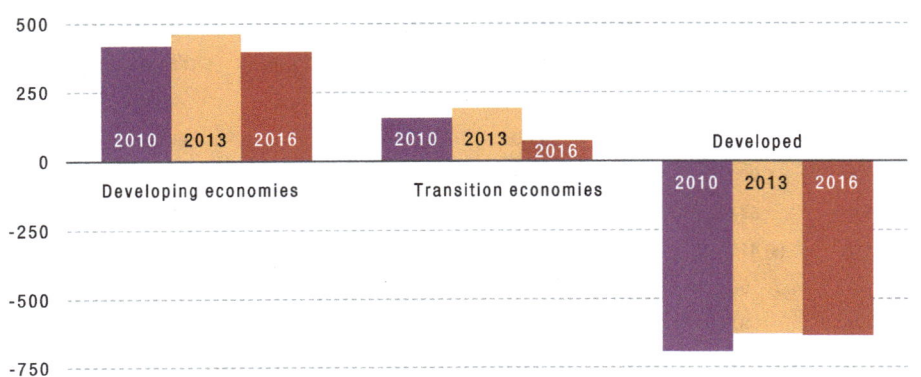

*Sum of the trade balances of individual economies, including intra-group trade.

World trade
declines
two years in a row

China,
the **United States of America** and **Germany**
account for
30%
of **global exports**

Transition
economies'
exports
down by
15% in
2016

The trade surpluses
of developing and
transition economies
declined
over the last
three years

Table 1.1.1 | Merchandise trade by group of economies

Group of economies	Exports			Imports			Trade balance	
	Value		Annual growth rate	Value		Annual growth rate	Value	Ratio to imports
	(Billions of US$)		(Percentage)	(Billions of US$)		(Percentage)	(Millions of US$)	(Percentage)
	2011	2016	2016	2011	2016	2016	2016	2016
World	**18 339**	**15 986**	**-3.0**	**18 416**	**16 150**	**-3.0**	**-164**	**-1.0**
Developing economies	7 899	6 988	-4.9	7 342	6 591	-5.7	397	6.0
Developing economies: Africa	611	349	-10.5	567	494	-10.9	-145	-29.4
Developing economies: America	1 111	886	-4.0	1 097	932	-9.5	-46	-4.9
Developing economies: Asia and Oceania	6 178	5 754	-4.7	5 678	5 166	-4.4	588	11.4
Transition economies	811	448	-14.6	587	376	-1.4	72	19.1
Developed economies	9 629	8 550	-0.7	10 486	9 183	-1.1	-633	-6.9
Selected groups								
Developing economies excluding China	6 001	4 891	-3.7	5 599	5 003	-5.7	-113	-2.3
Developing economies excluding LDCs	7 697	6 841	-5.0	7 133	6 373	-5.6	468	7.3
LDCs	203	147	-3.8	209	218	-7.8	-71	-32.6
LLDCs	221	141	-9.6	186	176	-6.7	-35	-19.7
SIDS (UNCTAD)	24	15	-17.9	36	34	-2.2	-19	-55.7
HIPCs (IMF)	119	101	-2.4	154	159	-7.3	-58	-36.7
BRICS	3 088	2 904	-8.0	2 893	2 374	-6.8	530	22.3
G20	10 909	9 691	-4.0	11 442	9 844	-3.9	-153	-1.6

Table 1.1.2 | Merchandise trade of least developed countries, main exporters

Economy[a]	Exports			Imports			Trade balance	
	Value		Annual growth rate	Value		Annual growth rate	Value	Ratio to imports
	(Millions of US$)		(Percentage)	(Millions of US$)		(Percentage)	(Millions of US$)	(Percentage)
	2011	2016	2016	2011	2016	2016	2016	2016
LDCs	**202 727**	**147 019**	**-3.8**	**209 431**	**218 247**	**-7.8**	**-71 228**	**-32.6**
LDCs: Africa and Haiti	147 942	84 032	-10.9	126 283	115 605	-15.3	-31 573	-27.3
Angola	67 310	27 306	-17.7	20 228	12 538	-39.4	14 768	117.8
Zambia	9 001	(e) 5 801	(e) -16.9	7 178	(e) 7 045	(e) -16.7	(e) -1 243	(e) -17.7
Dem. Rep. of the Congo	(e) 6 600	(e) 5 526	(e) -4.7	(e) 5 500	(e) 5 648	(e) -8.9	(e) -123	(e) -2.2
United Republic of Tanzania	4 735	5 172	4.9	10 799	9 488	-12.1	-4 316	-45.5
Equatorial Guinea	(e) 13 500	(e) 4 800	(e) -26.2	(e) 6 500	(e) 2 800	(e) -17.6	(e) 2 000	(e) 71.4
LDCs: Asia	54 241	62 450	7.7	81 530	100 538	2.5	-38 088	-37.9
Bangladesh	24 439	34 971	8.0	36 214	44 832	6.6	-9 861	-22.0
Myanmar	9 238	(e) 11 240	(e) -1.7	9 019	(e) 15 380	(e) -8.9	(e) -4 140	(e) -26.9
Cambodia	6 704	10 069	17.9	(e) 9 300	12 632	6.4	-2 562	-20.3
Lao People's Dem. Rep.	2 190	3 352	21.1	2 404	4 739	-9.4	-1 387	-29.3
Yemen	(e) 9 700	1 000	0.0	11 260	6 770	3.0	-5 770	-85.2
LDCs: Islands	545	537	8.5	1 619	2 104	-6.6	-1 566	-74.5
Solomon Islands	418	(e) 415	(e) 3.6	469	(e) 430	(e) -7.9	(e) -15	(e) -3.5
Vanuatu	67	50	28.2	304	422	15.0	-372	-88.2
Comoros	26	31	80.8	277	219	2.7	-189	-86.0
Timor-Leste	13	20	11.1	319	(e) 780	(e) -14.3	(e) -760	(e) -97.4
Kiribati	9	(e) 11	(e) 0.0	92	(e) 85	(e) -26.1	(e) -74	(e) -87.1

[a] Ranked by value of exports in 2016.

Table 1.1.3 | Leading exporters and importers in developing economies, by group of economies, 2016

Developing economies: Africa

Exporter (Ranked by value)	Value (Billions of US$)	Share in world total (Percentage)	Annual growth rate (Percentage)	Importer (Ranked by value)	Value (Billions of US$)	Share in world total (Percentage)	Annual growth rate (Percentage)
South Africa	75	0.47	-7.8	South Africa	(e) 92	(e) 0.57	(e) -12.5
Nigeria	33	0.21	-36.2	Egypt	56	0.35	-12.2
Algeria	29	0.18	-16.7	Algeria	47	0.29	-9.6
Angola	27	0.17	-17.7	Morocco	42	0.26	9.0
Egypt	25	0.16	19.3	Nigeria	39	0.24	-18.8
Developing Africa	**349**	**2.18**	**-10.5**	**Developing Africa**	**494**	**3.06**	**-10.9**

Developing economies: America

Exporter (Ranked by value)	Value (Billions of US$)	Share in world total (Percentage)	Annual growth rate (Percentage)	Importer (Ranked by value)	Value (Billions of US$)	Share in world total (Percentage)	Annual growth rate (Percentage)
Mexico	374	2.34	-1.7	Mexico	398	2.46	-1.9
Brazil	185	1.16	-3.1	Brazil	143	0.89	-19.8
Chile	61	0.38	-2.6	Chile	59	0.36	-5.9
Argentina	58	0.36	1.7	Argentina	56	0.34	-6.9
Peru	37	0.23	7.6	Colombia	45	0.28	-17.0
Developing America	**886**	**5.54**	**-4.0**	**Developing America**	**932**	**5.77**	**-9.5**

Developing economies: Asia and Oceania

Exporter (Ranked by value)	Value (Billions of US$)	Share in world total (Percentage)	Annual growth rate (Percentage)	Importer (Ranked by value)	Value (Billions of US$)	Share in world total (Percentage)	Annual growth rate (Percentage)
China	2 098	13.12	-7.7	China	1 588	9.83	-5.5
China, Hong Kong SAR	517	3.23	1.2	China, Hong Kong SAR	547	3.39	-2.2
Korea, Republic of	495	3.10	-5.9	Korea, Republic of	406	2.52	-6.9
Singapore	338	2.11	-2.5	India	360	2.23	-8.4
China, Taiwan Province of	280	1.75	-1.8	Singapore	292	1.81	-1.6
Developing Asia and Oceania	**5 754**	**35.99**	**-4.7**	**Developing Asia and Oceania**	**5 166**	**31.99**	**-4.4**

1.2 Trade structure by partner

Map 1.2 | **Main world import flows, 2016**
(Billions of United States dollars)

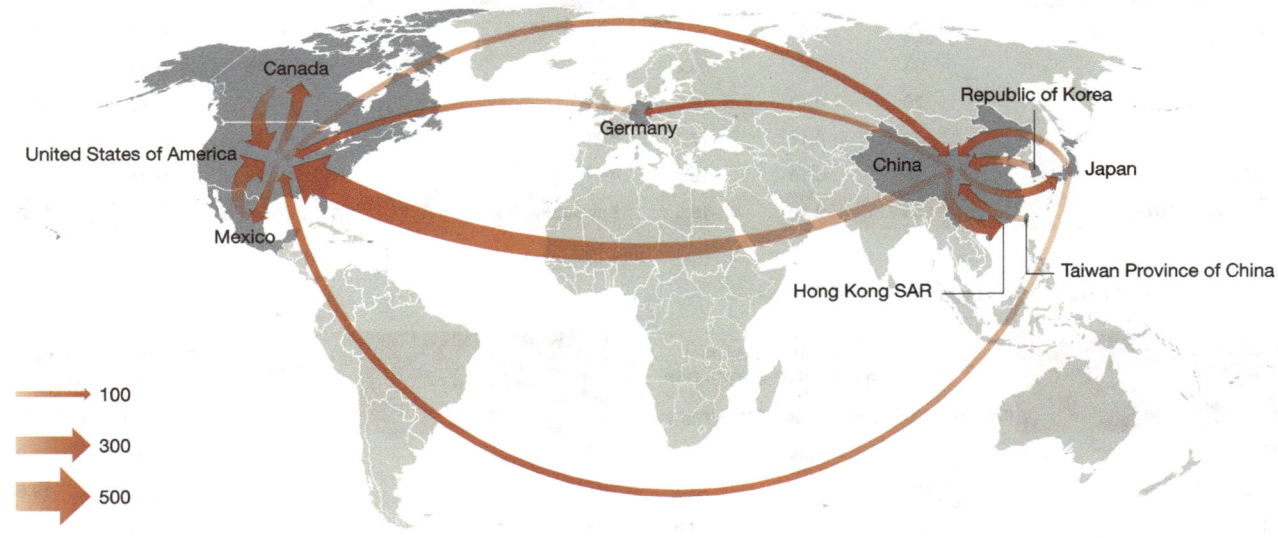

Note: Bilateral imports of US$100 billion or more are shown.

Concepts and definitions

Intra-trade is the trade between economies belonging to the same group. Extra-trade is the trade of economies of the same group with all economies outside the group. It represents the difference between a group's total trade and intra-trade.

In theory, the exports from an economy A to an economy B, should equal the imports of economy B from economy A recorded FOB. In practice, however, the values of both flows are often different. The reasons for these trade asymmetries comprise: different times of recording, different treatment of transit trade, underreporting, measurement errors and mis-pricing or mis-invoicing.

The exports to (imports from) all economies of the world do not always exactly add up to total exports (imports). The difference is caused by ship stores, bunkers and other exports of minor importance.

Shape of the global trade network

International merchandise trade flows are to a large extent transcontinental. In 2016, some of the largest flows ran between China, the United States of America, and Germany, jointly accounting for US$990 billion, 6 per cent of world imports. Considerable trade was recorded also between the United States of America and its neighbours, Canada and Mexico, as well as between mainland China and surrounding economies, including the Republic of Korea, Japan, Taiwan Province of China and Hong Kong Special Administrative Region of China (Hong Kong SAR).

In some regions, economies have developed stronger ties for mutual exchange of goods than in others. In 2016, in Europe more than two thirds and in Asia more than half of all exports were delivered to trading partners in the same region. In Oceania, Latin America and the Caribbean and in Africa this was the case for less than one fifth.

Figure 1.2.1 | **Intra- and extra-group exports, 2016**
(Percentage of total exports)

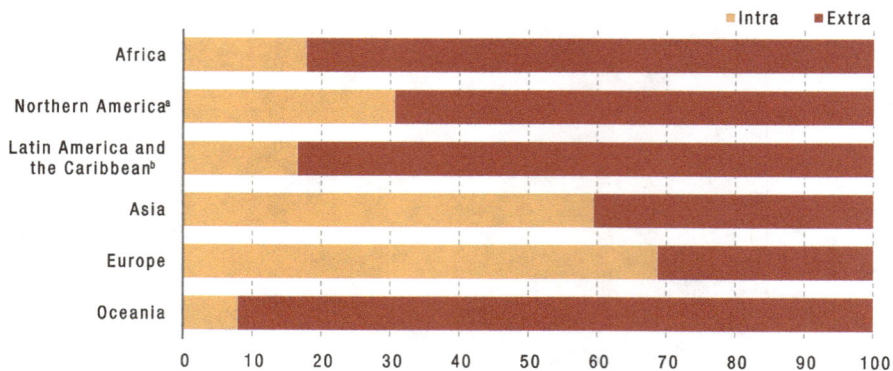

[a] Equal to the group 'Developed economies: America' on UNCTADstat.
[b] Equal to the group 'Developing economies: America' on UNCTADstat.

Trade within and between 'hemispheres'

Out of the total value of US$16.0 trillion of global merchandise trade, US$5.8 trillion, i.e. slightly more than one third, were accounted for by goods exchanged between different developed economies (North–North trade), while trade among developing and transition economies (South–South trade) accounted for US$4.3 trillion, i.e. slightly more than one quarter. The remaining US$5.7 trillion were comprised of exports from developed to developing and transition economies and in the opposite direction.

Figure 1.2.2 | Global trade flows, 2016

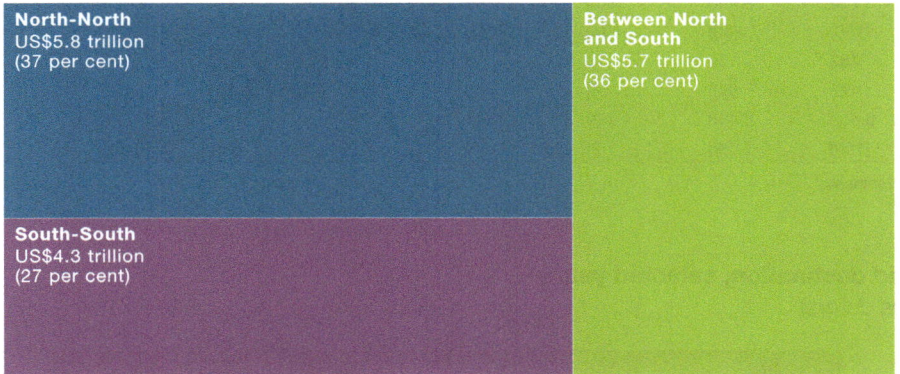

Note: North refers to developed economies; South, to developing and transition economies. Trade is measured from the export side.

With whom do developing economies mainly trade?

In 2016, developing economies delivered most of their exports to the United States of America (US$1.2 trillion), Japan (US$0.4 trillion) and to various developing economies in Asia, mainly China (US$ 0.9 trillion). These represented also the main origins of their imports. For LDCs, the main export markets also included some European economies. LDCs in Asia delivered the largest proportion of their exports to the United States of America, whereas for LDCs in Africa and Haiti the most important export destination was China.

Figure 1.2.3 | LDCs' main export destinations, 2016
(Billions of United States dollars)

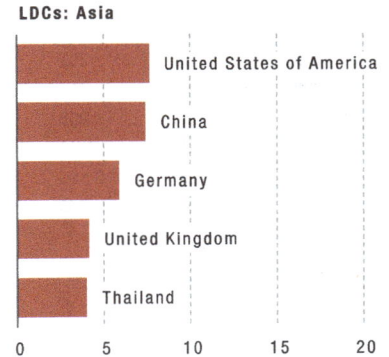

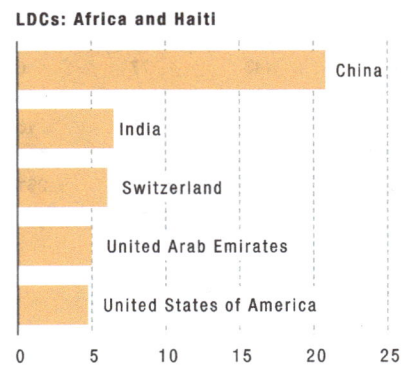

Flows between China, the United States of America and Germany make up 6% of global imports

69% of all European exports remain in Europe

South-South trade accounts for 27% of global exports

Exports of developing economies to the United States of America amount to US$1.2 trillion

Table 1.2.1 | **Exports by origin and destination, 2016**
(Billions of United States dollars)

Origin	Destination						
	World	Developing economies				Transition economies	Developed economies
		Total	Africa	America	Asia and Oceania		
World	**15 940**	**6 563**	**502**	**900**	**5 161**	**361**	**8 924**
	(100)	(41)	(3)	(6)	(32)	(2)	(56)
Developing economies	6 969	3 969	287	352	3 330	109	2 863
	(100)	(57)	(4)	(5)	(48)	(2)	(41)
Developing economies: Africa	350	178	62	8	108	2	164
	(100)	(51)	(18)	(2)	(31)	(1)	(47)
Developing economies: America	883	324	16	146	162	7	547
	(100)	(37)	(2)	(17)	(18)	(1)	(62)
Developing economies: Asia and Oceania	5 735	3 468	208	198	3 061	100	2 151
	(100)	(60)	(4)	(3)	(53)	(2)	(38)
Transition economies	452	135	16	6	113	81	235
	(100)	(30)	(4)	(1)	(25)	(18)	(52)
Developed economies	8 519	2 458	199	541	1 718	171	5 826
	(100)	(29)	(2)	(6)	(20)	(2)	(68)

Note: Percentage of exports to the whole world in parentheses.

Table 1.2.2 | **Exports by origin and destination, selected years**
(Billions of United States dollars)

Origin	Year	Destination						
		World	Developing economies				Transition economies	Developed economies
			Total	Africa	America	Asia and Oceania		
World	2006	12 117	3 849	301	596	2 953	316	7 893
	2011	18 328	7 279	581	1 080	5 619	564	10 275
	2016	15 940	6 563	502	900	5 161	361	8 924
Developing economies	2006	4 533	2 158	142	232	1 784	60	2 298
	2011	7 904	4 399	317	483	3 598	132	3 313
	2016	6 969	3 969	287	352	3 330	109	2 863
Developing economies: Africa	2006	362	109	33	12	64	1	248
	2011	619	270	82	26	163	3	330
	2016	350	178	62	8	108	2	164
Developing economies: America	2006	696	209	12	133	64	7	475
	2011	1 107	438	23	222	194	11	648
	2016	883	324	16	146	162	7	547
Developing economies: Asia and Oceania	2006	3 475	1 840	97	87	1 656	52	1 575
	2011	6 178	3 690	213	236	3 242	118	2 335
	2016	5 735	3 468	208	198	3 061	100	2 151
Transition economies	2006	443	77	6	7	64	84	281
	2011	809	174	13	11	149	151	411
	2016	452	135	16	6	113	81	235
Developed economies	2006	7 141	1 615	153	357	1 105	172	5 314
	2011	9 615	2 707	251	585	1 871	280	6 550
	2016	8 519	2 458	199	541	1 718	171	5 826

Table 1.2.3 | **Top destinations of developing economies' exports**

Destination (Ranked by value of exports)	Rank		2016		
	2016	2011	Value	Share in total exports	Cumulative share
			(Billions of US$)	(Percentage)	(Percentage)
United States	1	1	1 178	16.9	16.9
China	2	2	856	12.3	29.2
China, Hong Kong SAR	3	4	463	6.6	35.8
Japan	4	3	384	5.5	41.3
India	5	5	244	3.5	44.8
Korea, Republic of	6	6	237	3.4	48.2
Singapore	7	7	178	2.6	50.8
Germany	8	9	172	2.5	53.3
Viet Nam	9	22	161	2.3	55.6
Netherlands	10	10	152	2.2	57.8
United Kingdom	11	11	148	2.1	59.9
United Arab Emirates	12	16	134	1.9	61.8
China, Taiwan Province of	13	8	132	1.9	63.7
Malaysia	14	13	131	1.9	65.6
Thailand	15	17	122	1.7	67.3
Rest of the world	–	–	**2 276**	**32.7**	**100.0**
World	–	–	**6 969**	**100.0**	**100.0**

Table 1.2.4 | **Top origins of developing economies' imports**

Origin (Ranked by value of imports)	Rank		2016		
	2016	2011	Value	Share in total imports	Cumulative share
			(Billions of US$)	(Percentage)	(Percentage)
China	1	1	1 047	16.0	16.0
United States	2	2	733	11.2	27.2
Japan	3	3	457	7.0	34.2
Korea, Republic of	4	4	361	5.5	39.7
China, Taiwan Province of	5	6	289	4.4	44.1
Germany	6	5	282	4.3	48.5
Malaysia	7	8	174	2.7	51.1
India	8	11	155	2.4	53.5
Thailand	9	14	141	2.2	55.6
Australia	10	10	140	2.1	57.8
Singapore	11	9	138	2.1	59.9
France	12	15	128	2.0	61.9
Brazil	13	12	124	1.9	63.7
United Arab Emirates	14	13	122	1.9	65.6
Saudi Arabia	15	7	118	1.8	67.4
Rest of the world	–	–	**2 130**	**32.6**	**100.0**
World	–	–	**6 539**	**100.0**	**100.0**

1.3 Trade structure by product

Map 1.3 | Main export products, 2016

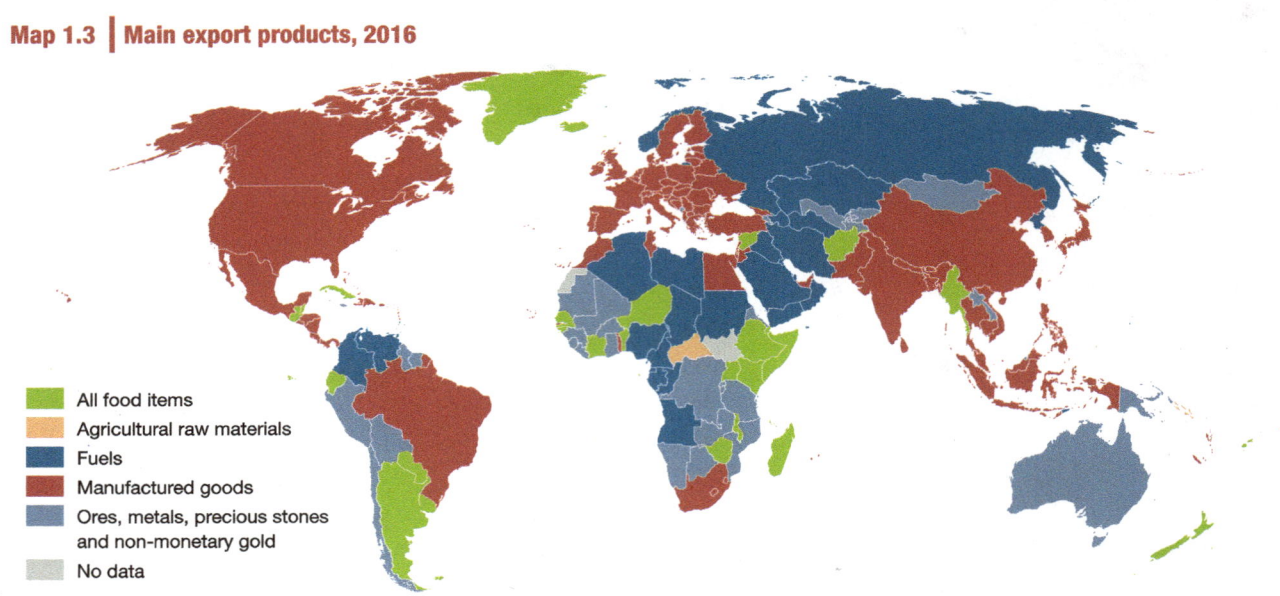

- All food items
- Agricultural raw materials
- Fuels
- Manufactured goods
- Ores, metals, precious stones and non-monetary gold
- No data

Concepts and definitions

The breakdown of merchandise trade by product group is based on the entries in the customs declarations that are coded in accordance with a globally harmonized classification system, called the Harmonized System. The values of the individual customs declarations have been summed up to the level of product group, error-checked and submitted to the United Nations Statistics Division for integration in the UN Comtrade database (United Nations, 2017a).

The UN Comtrade database contains product breakdowns based on the Standard International Trade Classification (SITC). These have been obtained by conversion of the raw data coded in Harmonized System and constitute the main source of the figures presented in this section. For correspondence between SITC codes and the five broad product groups presented in this section, see annex 6.2.

Regional specialization patterns

Economies have specialized their exports by different groups of products. In 2016, for many developed economies and developing economies in Southern and Eastern Asia, manufactured goods represented the most exported product group. Many transition economies and developing economies in Western Asia and North and Central Africa relied mainly on fuels. Food was strongly represented in the exports of some economies in South America and Eastern Africa; and ores, metals, precious stones and non-monetary gold in the exports of several Southern and Western African and Central Asian economies.

In developing economies, manufactured goods accounted for 72 percent of total exports – almost as much as in developed economies. In transition economies, only one third of exports were manufactured goods, while fuels accounted for almost one half.

Figure 1.3.1 | Export structure by product group, 2016
(Percentage)

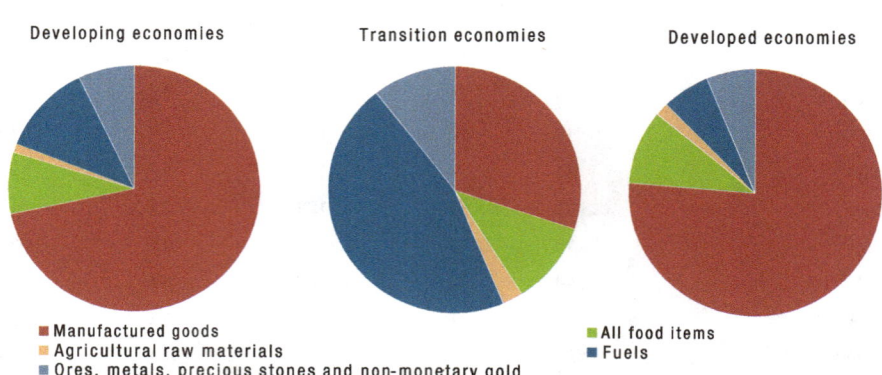

Developing economies   Transition economies   Developed economies

- Manufactured goods
- Agricultural raw materials
- Ores, metals, precious stones and non-monetary gold
- All food items
- Fuels

Decline in trade at the level of product groups

The continuing decrease in global trade in 2016 (see section 1.1) was reflected in negative annual growth rates particularly for trade in fuels. In 2016, global fuels exports reached only 80 per cent of their value in 2015. Trade in manufactured goods and agricultural raw materials decreased to a much smaller extent, by 2 per cent each. By contrast, trade in food recorded a slight increase (2 per cent), while trade in ores, metals, precious stones and non-monetary gold remained constant.

Figure 1.3.2 | **Annual growth rate of exports by product group, 2016** (Percentage)

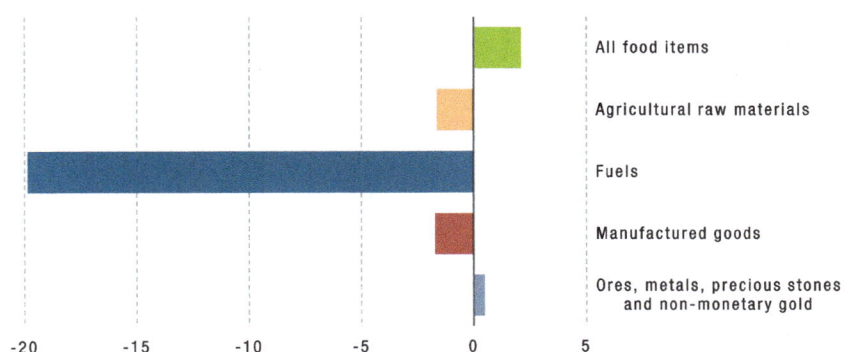

What do developing economies trade with others?

A breakdown of extra-trade by product group shows that developing economies in Africa and America imported much higher value of manufactured goods from the rest of the world than they exported. While in America this was offset by a positive balance in trade in food and in ores, metals, precious stones and non-monetary gold, in Africa it caused an overall extra-trade deficit. Extra-trade of developing economies in Asia and Oceania recorded a slight surplus resulting from higher exports of manufactured goods than imports.

Figure 1.3.3 | **Developing economies' extra-trade structure, 2016** (Percentage of exports)

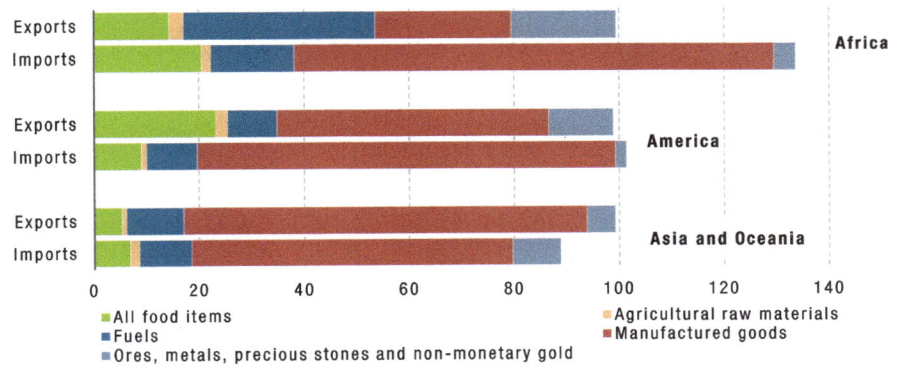

Many **developing** economies in **Africa** and in **America export mainly** primary goods

Fuels exports dropped by **20%** worldwide in 2016

Trade in **food increased** slightly: **+2%**

Africa's imports of **manufactured** goods more than **3 ½ times** higher than exports

Table 1.3 | **Exports by product group, origin and destination, 2016**
(Millions of United States dollars)*

All food items

Origin	Destination						
	World	Developing economies				Transition economies	Developed economies
		Total	Africa	America	Asia and Oceania		
World	**1 380 176**	**554 653**	**73 562**	**77 502**	**403 589**	**43 491**	**777 764**
	(100)	**(40)**	**(5)**	**(6)**	**(29)**	**(3)**	**(56)**
Developing economies	553 468	327 959	43 569	35 674	248 716	14 706	208 783
	(100)	(59)	(8)	(6)	(45)	(3)	(38)
Developing economies: Africa	49 887	25 415	12 648	417	12 350	1 335	22 978
	(100)	(51)	(25)	(1)	(25)	(3)	(46)
Developing economies: America	204 602	104 733	11 391	30 178	63 164	5 720	93 158
	(100)	(51)	(6)	(15)	(31)	(3)	(46)
Developing economies: Asia and Oceania	298 979	197 811	19 530	5 079	173 203	7 650	92 647
	(100)	(66)	(7)	(2)	(58)	(3)	(31)
Transition economies	44 483	19 180	4 771	219	14 190	14 682	10 563
	(100)	(43)	(11)	(0)	(32)	(33)	(24)
Developed economies	782 225	207 514	25 223	41 609	140 682	14 103	558 418
	(100)	(27)	(3)	(5)	(18)	(2)	(71)

* Percentage of exports to the whole world in parentheses.

Agricultural raw materials

Origin	Destination						
	World	Developing economies				Transition economies	Developed economies
		Total	Africa	America	Asia and Oceania		
World	**229 024**	**112 055**	**6 150**	**9 092**	**96 813**	**3 842**	**112 398**
	(100)	**(49)**	**(3)**	**(4)**	**(42)**	**(2)**	**(49)**
Developing economies	80 966	51 632	2 049	3 155	46 428	699	27 968
	(100)	(64)	(3)	(4)	(57)	(1)	(35)
Developing economies: Africa	9 631	6 072	865	103	5 105	61	3 477
	(100)	(63)	(9)	(1)	(53)	(1)	(36)
Developing economies: America	20 059	9 907	133	1 845	7 929	225	9 372
	(100)	(49)	(1)	(9)	(40)	(1)	(47)
Developing economies: Asia and Oceania	51 277	35 653	1 052	1 207	33 394	414	15 119
	(100)	(70)	(2)	(2)	(65)	(1)	(29)
Transition economies	10 748	5 856	250	96	5 510	1 088	3 796
	(100)	(54)	(2)	(1)	(51)	(10)	(35)
Developed economies	137 310	54 567	3 851	5 842	44 875	2 055	80 634
	(100)	(40)	(3)	(4)	(33)	(1)	(59)

* Percentage of exports to the whole world in parentheses.

Fuels

Origin	Destination						
	World	Developing economies				Transition economies	Developed economies
		Total	Africa	America	Asia and Oceania		
World	**1 510 936**	**724 647**	**56 406**	**88 482**	**579 759**	**22 544**	**732 237**
	(100)	(48)	(4)	(6)	(38)	(1)	(48)
Developing economies	831 134	540 648	36 192	31 179	473 276	867	286 151
	(100)	(65)	(4)	(4)	(57)	(0)	(34)
Developing economies: Africa	128 166	63 687	13 295	5 116	45 276	60	63 735
	(100)	(50)	(10)	(4)	(35)	(0)	(50)
Developing economies: America	82 408	42 656	570	21 315	20 772	7	39 223
	(100)	(52)	(1)	(26)	(25)	(0)	(48)
Developing economies: Asia and Oceania	620 560	434 304	22 327	4 749	407 229	800	183 194
	(100)	(70)	(4)	(1)	(66)	(0)	(30)
Transition economies	185 229	49 739	1 449	1 447	46 843	15 955	119 524
	(100)	(27)	(1)	(1)	(25)	(9)	(65)
Developed economies	494 572	134 260	18 764	55 856	59 640	5 721	326 561
	(100)	(27)	(4)	(11)	(12)	(1)	(66)

* Percentage of exports to the whole world in parentheses.

Manufactured goods

Origin	Destination						
	World	Developing economies				Transition economies	Developed economies
		Total	Africa	America	Asia and Oceania		
World	**11 255 836**	**4 449 802**	**334 055**	**671 515**	**3 444 232**	**271 448**	**6 515 312**
	(100)	(40)	(3)	(6)	(31)	(2)	(58)
Developing economies	4 956 927	2 719 183	190 063	269 639	2 259 481	90 262	2 136 481
	(100)	(55)	(4)	(5)	(46)	(2)	(43)
Developing economies: Africa	90 854	44 224	28 222	1 932	14 071	388	45 467
	(100)	(49)	(31)	(2)	(16)	(0)	(50)
Developing economies: America	457 614	110 190	2 985	86 506	20 699	516	346 192
	(100)	(24)	(1)	(19)	(5)	(0)	(76)
Developing economies: Asia and Oceania	4 408 458	2 564 769	158 856	181 201	2 224 712	89 358	1 744 822
	(100)	(58)	(4)	(4)	(51)	(2)	(40)
Transition economies	121 643	34 413	4 773	4 183	25 458	39 463	47 717
	(100)	(28)	(4)	(3)	(21)	(32)	(39)
Developed economies	6 177 266	1 696 205	139 219	397 694	1 159 293	141 723	4 331 113
	(100)	(28)	(2)	(6)	(19)	(2)	(70)

* Percentage of exports to the whole world in parentheses.

Ores, metals, precious stones and non-monetary gold

Origin	Destination						
	World	Developing economies				Transition economies	Developed economies
		Total	Africa	America	Asia and Oceania		
World	**1 054 248**	**531 038**	**17 228**	**19 307**	**494 503**	**9 049**	**502 611**
	(100)	(50)	(2)	(2)	(47)	(1)	(48)
Developing economies	495 742	300 805	12 075	8 127	280 603	1 672	186 379
	(100)	(61)	(2)	(2)	(57)	(0)	(38)
Developing economies: Africa	70 074	38 077	6 992	388	30 697	352	28 195
	(100)	(54)	(10)	(1)	(44)	(1)	(40)
Developing economies: America	109 401	55 417	784	5 784	48 849	395	53 235
	(100)	(51)	(1)	(5)	(45)	(0)	(49)
Developing economies: Asia and Oceania	316 266	207 311	4 299	1 955	201 057	925	104 949
	(100)	(66)	(1)	(1)	(64)	(0)	(33)
Transition economies	43 123	12 086	356	164	11 566	4 694	26 343
	(100)	(28)	(1)	(0)	(27)	(11)	(61)
Developed economies	515 383	218 148	4 797	11 016	202 334	2 683	289 888
	(100)	(42)	(1)	(2)	(39)	(1)	(56)

* Percentage of exports to the whole world in parentheses.

1.4 Trade indicators

Map 1.4 | **Product concentration index of exports, 2016**

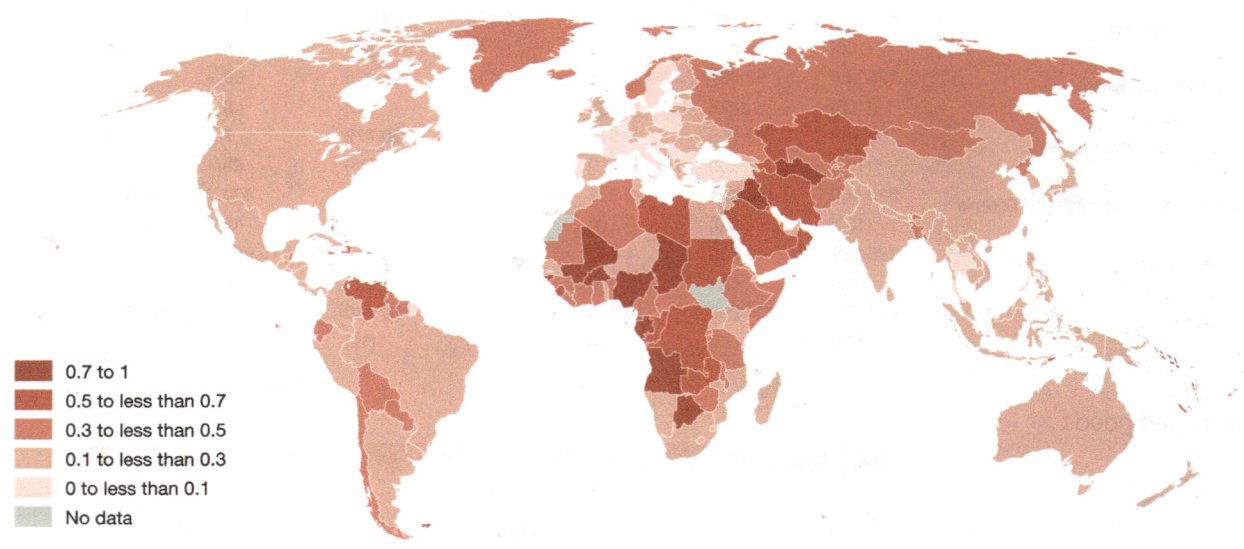

- 0.7 to 1
- 0.5 to less than 0.7
- 0.3 to less than 0.5
- 0.1 to less than 0.3
- 0 to less than 0.1
- No data

Note: This index measures the extent to which a large share of exports is accounted for by a small number of product groups. The index has a value of 1 when an economy exports only one group of products and a value of 0 if all product groups are equally represented.

Concepts and definitions

This section presents different indices that can be used to analyze trade flows and trade patterns, for example, from the perspective of relative competitiveness, the structure of global exports and imports markets, or the importance of trade for the economy, both for individual economies and for groups of economies, over time.

Information on how the indices in this section are calculated is provided in annex 6.3. The indices represent a subset of the trade indices contained in UNCTADstat (UNCTAD 2017a).

How concentrated was the structure of exports?

In 2016, in African developing economies and transition economies, merchandise exports were generally more concentrated on fewer product groups than elsewhere. The export structure of European economies was comparatively dispersed. All in all, the geographic distribution of the product concentration index appears correlated with the distribution of mainly fuel exporting economies (see section 1.3).

How did the prices of exports and imports develop?

From 2000 to 2016, the terms of trade – the ratio between the prices of exports and imports – remained almost constant in developed economies and increased slightly and steadily (by 17 per cent) in developing ones. LDCs in Africa and Haiti and transition economies registered decreasing terms of trade over the last four years.

Figure 1.4.1 | **Terms of trade index**
(2000=100)

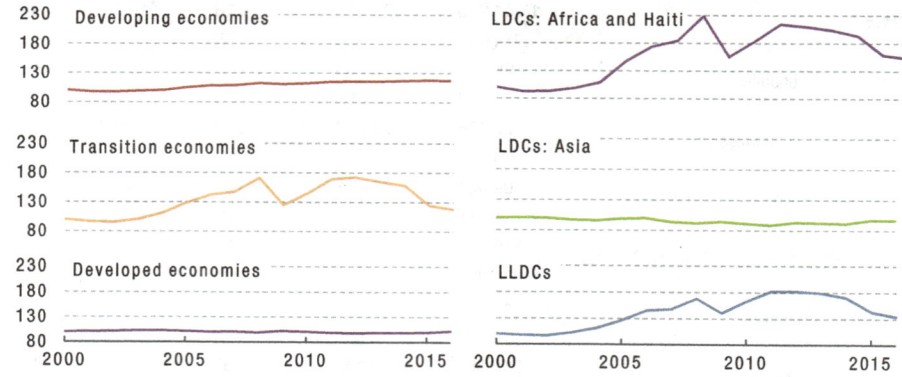

Note: This index indicates by how much the relative price between exports and imports has increased in relation to the base year.

How concentrated is global product supply?

The degree to which a large proportion of world exports originate from a small number of economies differs considerably across product groups. Exports of manufactured goods are more cumulated among few suppliers than other types of products, as indicated by a relatively high market concentration index, standing at 0.20 in 2016. This is due to an increase of the index from 2004 to 2015. In the same period the market concentration indices of food and agricultural raw materials fell.

Figure 1.4.2 | Market concentration index of exports

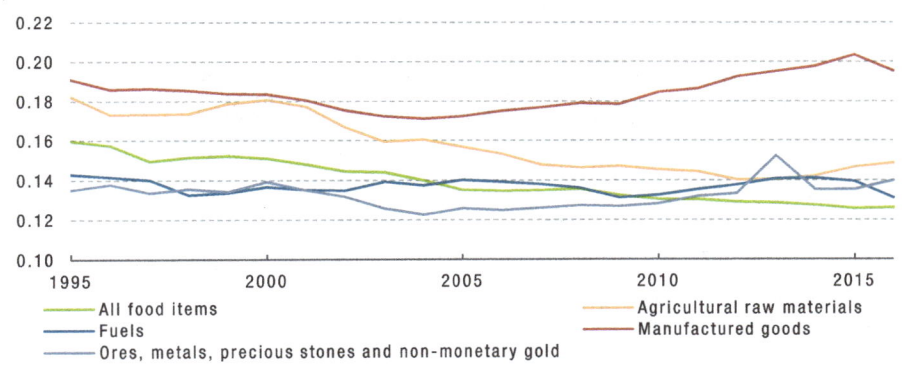

Note: This index measures the extent to which a high proportion of exports are delivered by a small number of economies. It has a value of 1 if all exports originate from a single economy.

How important is trade for economies?

Over the last ten years, the importance of trade in goods relative to domestic economic output has declined significantly in developing and transition economies. In developing economies, trade openness, measured as the ratio between the average of exports and imports of goods to GDP, fell from 31 per cent in 2006 to 22 per cent in 2016. In transition economies the rate decreased from 27 to 22 per cent. Trade openness of developed economies has been comparatively low. After a peak around the year 2011, in 2016 the rate amounted to 19 per cent, the same level as in 2006.

Figure 1.4.3 | Trade openness index
(Percentage)

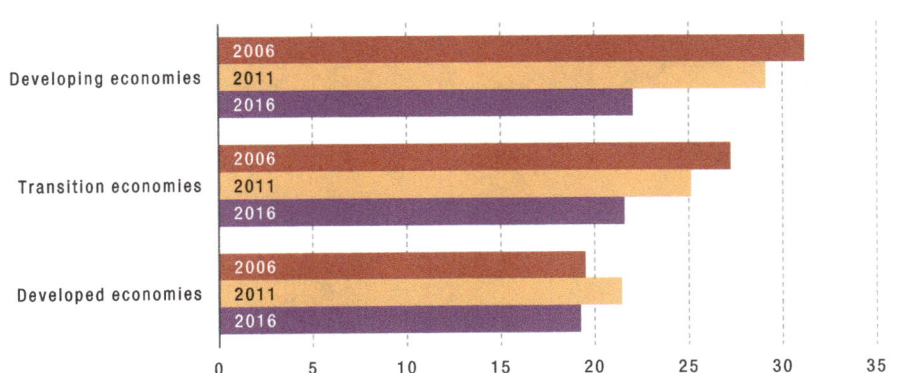

Note: This index measures the relative importance of international trade in goods relative to the domestic economic output of an economy. Exports are given equal weight to imports.

Transition economies and **African** developing economies have **narrowest range** of **export products**

Terms of trade of **developing** economies have **improved by 17%** since 2000

The global **supply** of **agricultural** products has become **less concentrated** over the last 15 years

Trade openness is **declining** in developing and transition economies

Table 1.4.1 | **Selected trade indices by group of economies**
(2000=100)

Developing economies

Year	Volume[a]		Purchasing power of exports[b]	Terms of trade[c]
	Imports	Exports		
2006	179	179	177	108
2011	234	256	228	115
2015	266	295	252	118
2016	274	298	255	117

Developing economies: Africa

Year	Volume[a]		Purchasing power of exports[b]	Terms of trade[c]
	Imports	Exports		
2006	146	193	184	143
2011	163	291	222	192
2015	198	388	180	163
2016	205	371	170	154

[a] This index indicates the change in exports or imports, adjusted for the movement of prices, relative to the base year.
[b] This index indicates the change in exports, valuated in prices of imports, relative to the base year.
[c] See note, figure 1.4.1 above.

Developing economies: America

Year	Volume[a]		Purchasing power of exports[b]	Terms of trade[c]
	Imports	Exports		
2006	130	142	152	128
2011	149	203	190	154
2015	168	213	172	129
2016	172	204	173	127

Developing economies: Asia and Oceania

Year	Volume[a]		Purchasing power of exports[b]	Terms of trade[c]
	Imports	Exports		
2006	194	186	183	101
2011	264	264	239	102
2015	298	305	279	109
2016	307	313	284	109

[a] This index indicates the change in exports or imports, adjusted for the movement of prices, relative to the base year.
[b] This index indicates the change in exports, valuated in prices of imports, relative to the base year.
[c] See note, figure 1.4.1 above.

Transition economies

Year	Volume[a]		Purchasing power of exports[b]	Terms of trade[c]
	Imports	Exports		
2006	164	267	227	142
2011	189	384	301	169
2015	197	300	226	125
2016	194	322	209	118

Developed economies

Year	Volume[a]		Purchasing power of exports[b]	Terms of trade[c]
	Imports	Exports		
2006	124	127	122	100
2011	132	129	126	99
2015	142	138	135	100
2016	144	142	139	102

[a] This index indicates the change in exports or imports, adjusted for the movement of prices, relative to the base year.
[b] This index indicates the change in exports, valuated in prices of imports, relative to the base year.
[c] See note, figure 1.4.1 above.

Table 1.4.2 | **Selected trade indices, landlocked developing countries**
(2000=100)

Economy	Volume[a]				Purchasing power of exports[b]		Terms of trade[c]	
	Imports		Exports					
	2011	2016	2011	2016	2011	2016	2011	2016
Afghanistan	105	185	307	382	152	299	145	161
Armenia	200	356	265	267	256	438	128	123
Azerbaijan	573	497	482	504	1 098	497	192	100
Bhutan	241	284	298	364	327	324	136	114
Bolivia (Plurinational State of)	226	279	300	196	471	241	209	86
Botswana	151	202	200	198	126	185	84	91
Burkina Faso	446	562	217	368	634	814	142	145
Burundi	85	98	286	289	139	152	164	155
Central African Republic	74	44	126	191	56	34	76	77
Chad	690	515	598	467	1 506	588	218	114
Ethiopia	231	302	399	935	335	427	145	141
Kazakhstan	242	214	432	348	565	288	233	135
Kyrgyzstan	143	136	345	400	175	166	122	122
Lao People's Dem. Rep.	310	668	238	571	351	654	113	98
Lesotho	447	360	192	173	329	306	74	85
Malawi	203	162	251	262	207	192	102	119
Mali	118	167	207	267	217	286	184	171
Mongolia	202	356	525	337	440	567	218	159
Nepal	66	55	153	298	48	47	72	85
Niger	133	149	304	330	242	232	182	156
Paraguay	237	238	316	283	204	253	86	106
Republic of Moldova	351	457	378	401	266	335	76	73
Rwanda	272	530	549	724	503	945	185	178
Swaziland	93	89	91	82	102	105	110	118
Tajikistan	68	76	205	345	69	67	101	89
TFYR of Macedonia	173	217	150	187	151	210	88	97
Turkmenistan	147	263	271	286	331	320	226	122
Uganda	241	350	200	226	292	429	121	122
Uzbekistan	153	165	236	313	286	261	187	158
Zambia	262	268	437	551	545	451	208	169
Zimbabwe	72	72	102	106	78	78	109	109

[a] This index indicates the change in exports or imports, adjusted for the movement of prices, relative to the base year.
[b] This index indicates the change in exports, valuated in prices of imports, relative to the base year.
[c] See note, figure 1.4.1 above.

International trade in services

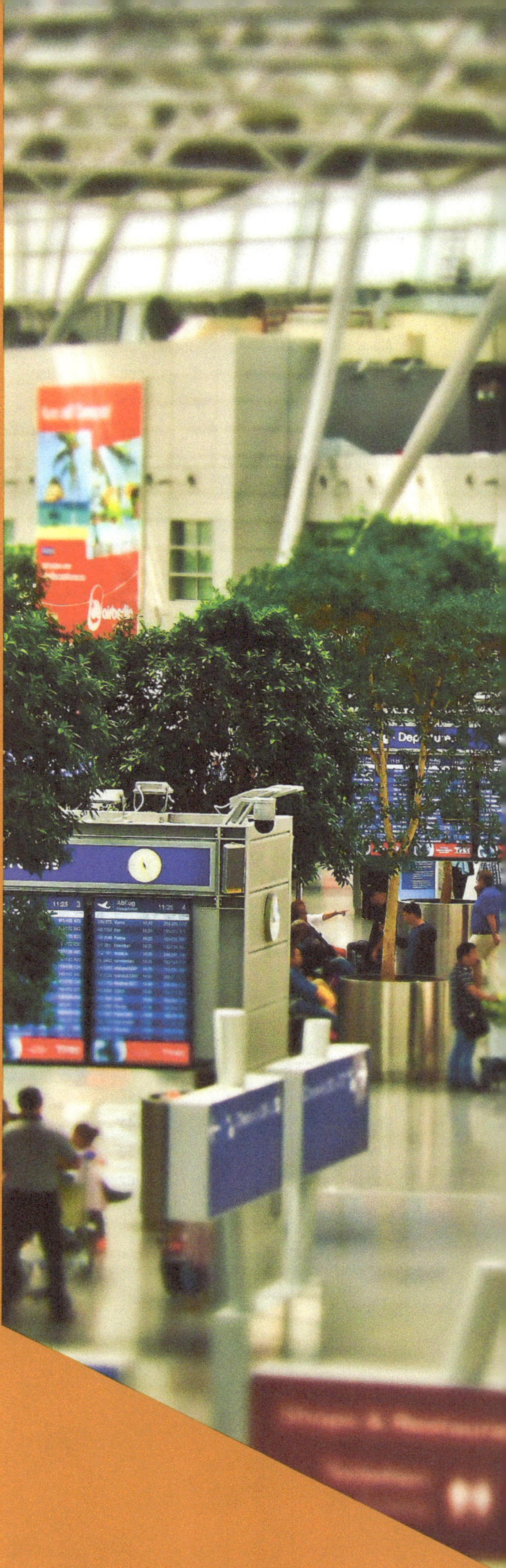

KEY FIGURES 2016

Growth of global trade in services

+0.4%

Value of world services exports

US$4.9 trillion

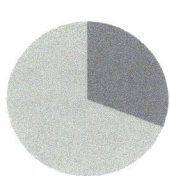

Developing economies' share in world exports

29%

Share of travel in services exports

25%

2.1 Total trade in services

Map 2.1 | **Exports of services, 2016**

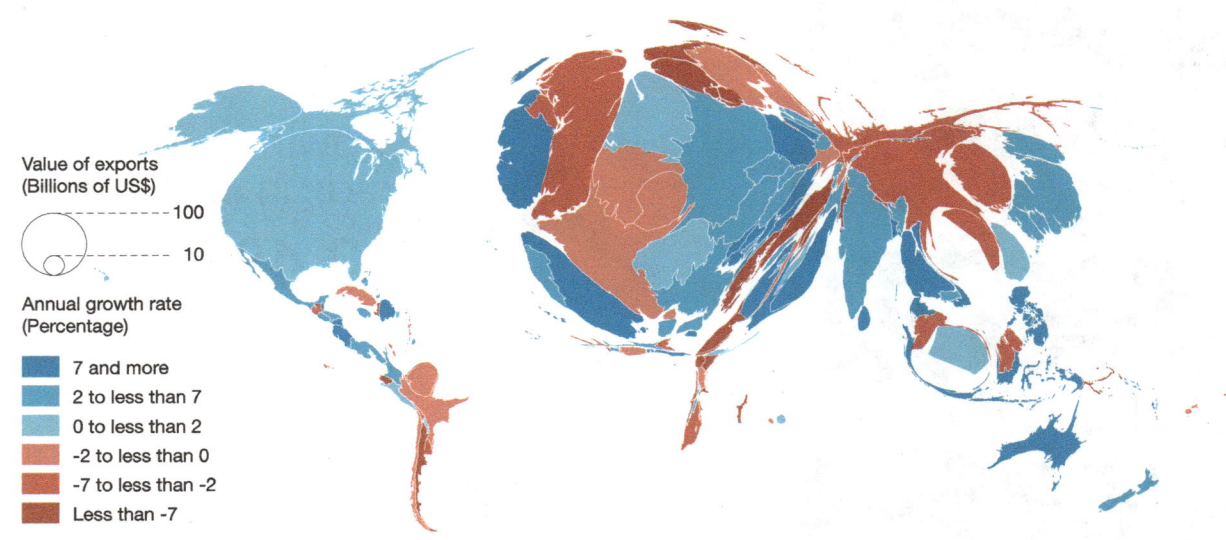

Value of exports
(Billions of US$)

- - - - - - - 100

- - - - - - 10

Annual growth rate
(Percentage)

- 7 and more
- 2 to less than 7
- 0 to less than 2
- -2 to less than 0
- -7 to less than -2
- Less than -7

Concepts and definitions

In this chapter, in accordance with the concepts of the balance of payments (International Monetary Fund, 2009) and of the national accounts (United Nations et al., 2009), services are understood as the result of a production activity that changes the conditions of the consuming units, or facilitates the exchange of products or financial assets. Services are not generally separate items over which ownership rights can be established. They cannot generally be separated from their production.

Trade in services, as represented by the data in this chapter, takes place when a service is supplied in any of the following modes: from one economy to another (services cross the border); within an economy to a service consumer of another economy (consumer crosses the border); through the presence of natural persons of one economy in another economy (supplier crosses the border) (United Nations et al., 2012).

Stagnation in world services trade

World services exports reached US$4.9 trillion in 2016, one third of the value of merchandise exports. Thereby global trade in services remained stagnant for two years, after a period of steady growth from 2009 to 2014.

Services exports come mainly from developed economies. These together accounted for two thirds of total services exports. However, several Asian developing economies also played an important role. The top five Asian developing economies captured almost 15 per cent of the world market share in 2016, the same share as all other developing economies combined.

Many economies in Africa and South America, where services exports had already been low, recorded a further decrease in 2016.

Figure 2.1.1 | **World services exports**
(Trillions of United States dollars)

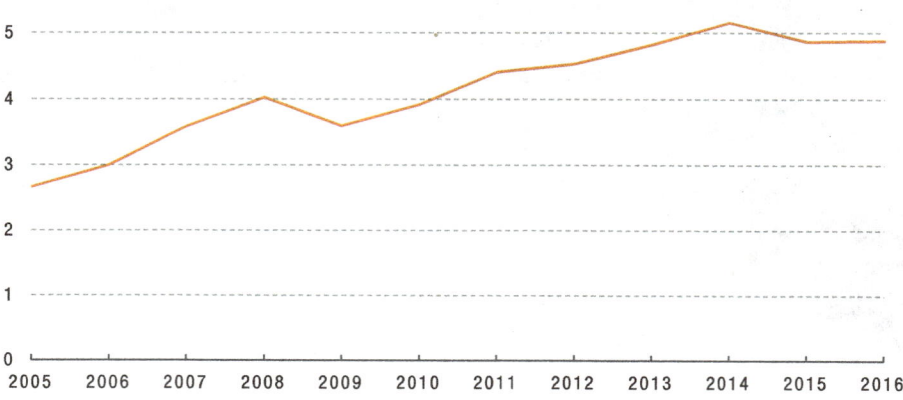

Strong slowdown in Africa and transition economies

A review of the changes in exports and imports by development status and region in 2016 reveals a diverse picture. Services imports dropped dramatically in transition economies (-11 per cent). Also African (-10 per cent) and, to a lesser extent, American (-4 per cent) developing economies recorded a strong decrease. In Africa this fall was accompanied by a considerable reduction of exports (-6 per cent). Developed economies, in contrast to developing ones, recorded rising services imports and exports.

Figure 2.1.2 | **Services trade annual growth rates, 2016**
(Percentage)

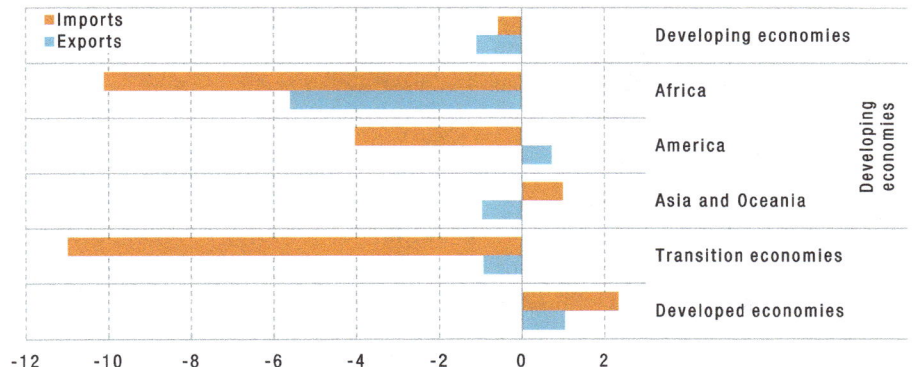

Leading services exporters

The world's top services exporter in 2016 was the United States of America, with US$752 billion worth of services sold internationally, representing 15 per cent of global exports, followed by four European Union member States that jointly took one fifth of the world market. Among developing economies, the main players in services trade were located in Asia, led by China (US$208 billion) and India (US$162 billion). China's services exports were greater than those of the Netherlands, at number five among developed economies.

Figure 2.1.3 | **Top services exporters, 2016**
(Billions of United States dollars)

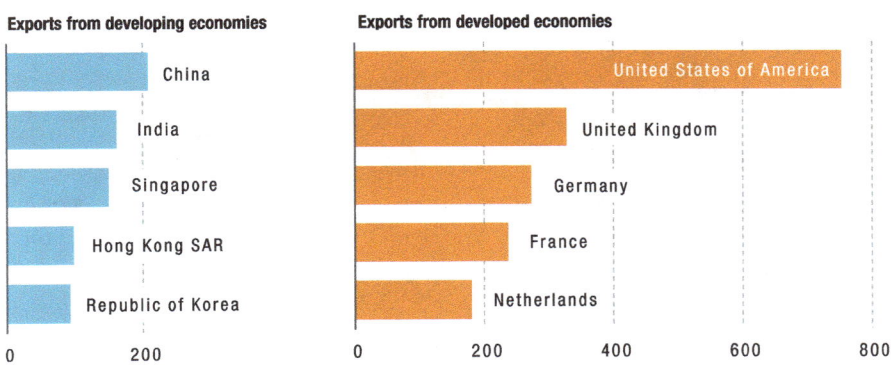

Global
trade in services stagnant for
two consecutive years

**Five
Asian economies**
account for **half** of
services exports
from
developing
economies

**African
services** imports
fell by **10%** in 2016

The **United States
of America** supplied
services worth
US$752 billion
to other economies

Table 2.1.1 | **Trade in services by group of economies**

Group of economies	Exports				Imports			
	Value (Billions of US$)		Share in world (Percentage)	Annual growth rate (Percentage)	Value (Billions of US$)		Share in world (Percentage)	Annual growth rate (Percentage)
	2011	2016	2016	2016	2011	2016	2016	2016
World	**4 406**	**4 879**	**100.0**	**0.4**	**4 281**	**4 797**	**100.0**	**0.8**
Developing economies	1 242	1 436	29.4	-1.1	1 525	1 818	37.9	-0.6
Developing economies: Africa	98	96	2.0	-5.6	171	144	3.0	-10.1
Developing economies: America	154	171	3.5	0.7	210	203	4.2	-4.0
Developing economies: Asia and Oceania	989	1 169	24.0	-1.0	1 144	1 471	30.7	1.0
Transition economies	116	107	2.2	-0.9	143	126	2.6	-11.0
Developed economies	3 048	3 337	68.4	1.0	2 613	2 853	59.5	2.3
Selected groups								
Developing economies excluding China	1 041	1 227	25.2	-0.5	1 277	1 365	28.4	-2.0
Developing economies excluding LDCs	1 212	1 399	28.7	-1.0	1 451	1 749	36.5	-0.3
LDCs	30	36	0.7	-3.6	74	69	1.4	-5.9
LLDCs	34	37	0.8	-5.0	51	56	1.2	-3.6
SIDS (UNCTAD)	18	20	0.4	1.2	16	14	0.3	-3.2
HIPCs (IMF)	30	35	0.7	-3.4	51	55	1.1	-4.7
BRICS	452	469	9.6	-1.2	560	740	15.4	0.8
G20	2 455	2 675	54.8	-0.4	2 435	2 718	56.7	0.5

Table 2.1.2 | **Leading services exporters and importers by group of economies, 2016**

Developing economies: Africa

Exporter (Ranked by value)	Value (Billions of US$)	Share in world total (Percentage)	Annual growth rate (Percentage)	Importer (Ranked by value)	Value (Billions of US$)	Share in world total (Percentage)	Annual growth rate (Percentage)
Morocco	15	0.32	4.8	Egypt	(e) 17	(e) 0.35	(e) -2.8
South Africa	14	0.29	-4.6	South Africa	15	0.31	-3.7
Egypt	(e) 14	(e) 0.29	(e) -22.8	Angola	(e) 13	(e) 0.26	(e) -27.4
Ghana	(e) 6	(e) 0.12	(e) -0.9	Nigeria	(e) 12	(e) 0.26	(e) -38.5
Kenya	(e) 4	(e) 0.08	(e) -11.3	Algeria	(e) 11	(e) 0.23	(e) -2.3
Developing Africa	**96**	**1.96**	**-5.6**	**Developing Africa**	**144**	**3.01**	**-10.1**

Developing economies: America

Exporter (Ranked by value)	Value (Billions of US$)	Share in world total (Percentage)	Annual growth rate (Percentage)	Importer (Ranked by value)	Value (Billions of US$)	Share in world total (Percentage)	Annual growth rate (Percentage)
Brazil	(e) 33	(e) 0.68	(e) -1.4	Brazil	(e) 64	(e) 1.33	(e) -9.8
Mexico	24	0.49	5.3	Mexico	32	0.67	-0.4
Argentina	(e) 13	(e) 0.26	(e) -8.9	Argentina	(e) 20	(e) 0.41	(e) 10.3
Panama	(e) 12	(e) 0.25	(e) 2.0	Chile	(e) 13	(e) 0.27	(e) -3.8
Cuba	(e) 11	(e) 0.23	(e) -1.1	Venezuela (Bolivarian Rep. of)	-	-	-
Developing America	**171**	**3.51**	**0.7**	**Developing America**	**203**	**4.23**	**-4.0**

Developing economies: Asia and Oceania

Exporter (Ranked by value)	Value (Billions of US$)	Share in world total (Percentage)	Annual growth rate (Percentage)
China	208	4.27	-4.2
India	(e) 162	(e) 3.32	(e) 3.6
Singapore	150	3.07	0.7
China, Hong Kong SAR	(e) 98	(e) 2.02	(e) -5.7
Korea, Republic of	93	1.90	-5.0
Developing Asia and Oceania	**1 169**	**23.96**	**-1.0**

Importer (Ranked by value)	Value (Billions of US$)	Share in world total (Percentage)	Annual growth rate (Percentage)
China	453	9.44	3.9
Singapore	156	3.24	0.7
India	(e) 134	(e) 2.79	(e) 8.2
Korea, Republic of	110	2.30	-2.0
United Arab Emirates	83	1.73	2.8
Developing Asia and Oceania	**1 471**	**30.65**	**1.0**

Transition economies

Exporter (Ranked by value)	Value (Billions of US$)	Share in world total (Percentage)	Annual growth rate (Percentage)
Russian Federation	51	1.04	-2.3
Ukraine	(e) 12	(e) 0.25	(e) -0.4
Belarus	7	0.14	2.7
Kazakhstan	(e) 6	(e) 0.13	(e) -2.4
Serbia	(e) 6	(e) 0.13	(e) 7.3
Transition economies	**107**	**2.19**	**-0.9**

Importer (Ranked by value)	Value (Billions of US$)	Share in world total (Percentage)	Annual growth rate (Percentage)
Russian Federation	74	1.55	-16.1
Ukraine	(e) 11	(e) 0.23	(e) 4.6
Kazakhstan	(e) 11	(e) 0.23	(e) -4.6
Azerbaijan	(e) 8	(e) 0.16	(e) -13.2
Serbia	(e) 5	(e) 0.10	(e) 2.7
Transition economies	**126**	**2.64**	**-11.0**

Developed economies

Exporter (Ranked by value)	Value (Billions of US$)	Share in world total (Percentage)	Annual growth rate (Percentage)
United States	(e) 752	(e) 15.42	(e) 0.2
United Kingdom	(e) 327	(e) 6.71	(e) -5.0
Germany	(e) 273	(e) 5.59	(e) 3.1
France	(e) 237	(e) 4.85	(e) -2.0
Netherlands	(e) 180	(e) 3.68	(e) 1.0
Developed economies	**3 337**	**68.38**	**1.0**

Importer (Ranked by value)	Value (Billions of US$)	Share in world total (Percentage)	Annual growth rate (Percentage)
United States	(e) 503	(e) 10.49	(e) 2.9
Germany	(e) 312	(e) 6.51	(e) 4.3
France	(e) 236	(e) 4.91	(e) 1.7
United Kingdom	(e) 199	(e) 4.14	(e) -5.6
Ireland	(e) 192	(e) 4.00	(e) 14.6
Developed economies	**2 853**	**59.48**	**2.3**

2.2 Trade in services by category

Map 2.2 | **Changes in services exports by category, 2011–2016**
(Average annual growth rate, percentage)

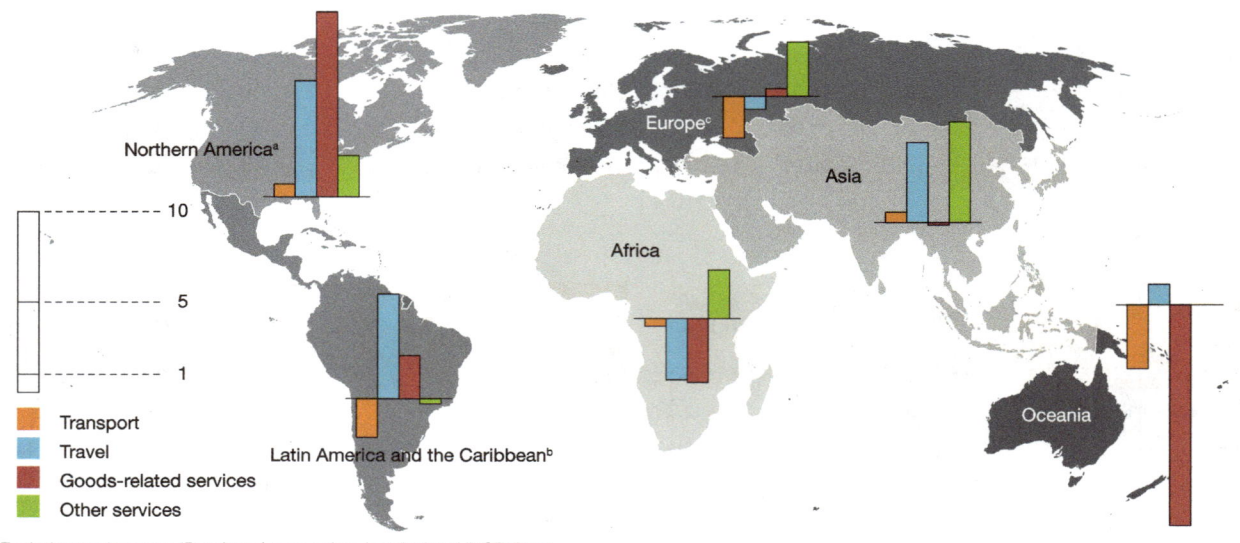

a Equivalent to the group 'Developed economies: America' on UNCTADstat.
b Equivalent to the group 'Developing economies: America' on UNCTADstat.
c Incl. the Russian Federation and the French overseas departments.

Concepts and definitions

The breakdown by service category in this section corresponds to the division of services in the balance of payments statistics (United Nations et al., 2012). The concepts of selected main categories are outlined below:

- Transport: covers international transport of goods and passengers.

- Travel: includes all goods and services consumed by travelers outside their country of residence; does not include international transport of passengers.

- Goods-related services: comprise processing and packaging of goods and their repair and maintenance.

- Other services: is a heterogeneous group encompassing, among other categories, construction, insurance and financial services, telecommunications and computer services, various business, professional, and technical services, and intellectual property charges.

For further details, see annex 6.2.

Regional trends

Over the last five years, exports of transport, travel, goods-related and other services developed differently in the various regions of the world. For example, exports of travel increased strongly in Northern America, in Latin America and the Caribbean and in Asia, whereas they fell in Africa and Europe. Exports of the group 'other services' increased in most regions of the world, particularly in Asia.

Figure 2.2.1 | **Structure of services exports, 2016**

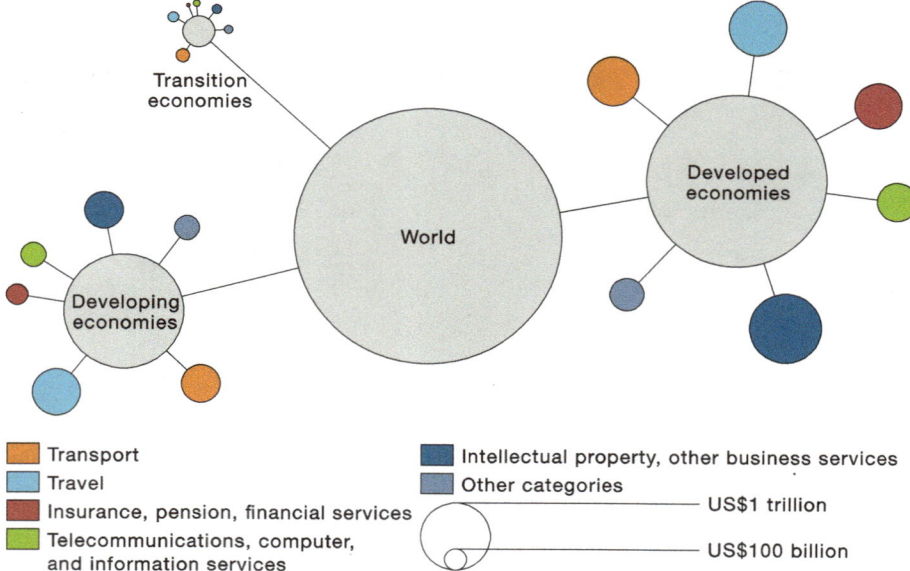

Note: For the grouping of service categories, see annex 6.2.

Structure by group of economies and category in 2016

In 2016, travel constituted an important category of services exported by developing economies, accounting on average for one third of their total services exports. Developing economies exported travel services to non-residents worth almost half a trillion United States dollars. That segment was thereby of equal size as exports of insurance, pension and financial services by developed economies. Travel has been growing over recent years, driven in particular by trends in Latin America and the Caribbean and in Asia.

The services exports of developed economies were dominated by business services such as research and development, consulting, technical and trade-related services and charges on intellectual property, jointly accounting for around US$1 trillion, while exports of travel came second (US$700 billion).

Figure 2.2.2 | **Annual growth rate of services exports*, 2016**
(Percentage)

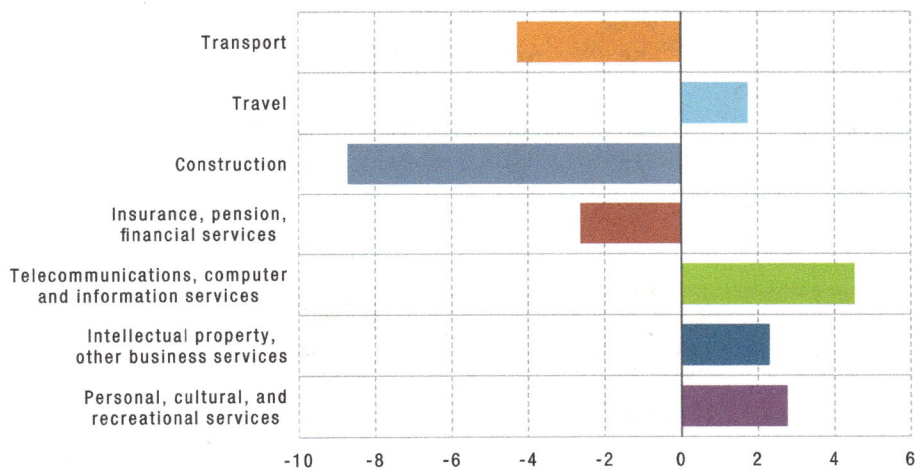

* Selected categories.
Note: For the grouping of service categories, see annex 6.2.

Global trends in 2016

The stagnation of global trade in total services in 2016 (see section 2.1) masks notable changes at the level of individual service categories. Telecommunications, computer and information services showed a relatively strong increase (4.5 per cent). Exports of intellectual property and other business services as well as of personal, cultural and recreational services recorded positive growth rates, ranging between 2 and 3 per cent. Travel receipts increased by modest 1.8 per cent. Meanwhile, trade in international transport (-4.3 per cent) and in insurance, pension and financial services (-2.6 per cent), two service groups strongly linked with merchandise trade, declined. 2016 was a particularly unfavorable year for trade in construction, recording a drop of 8.7 per cent.

Average annual growth of Africa's international travel receipts over the last 5 years: -3.5%

Developing economies exported travel services worth US$477 billion

Global exports of telecommunications, computer and information services increased by 4.5%

Falling exports of transport services: -4.3%

Table 2.2.1 | **Trade in services by service category and by group of economies**

Developing economies

Service category	Exports			Imports		
	Value		Annual growth rate	Value		Annual growth rate
	(Billions of US$)		(Percentage)	(Billions of US$)		(Percentage)
	2011	2016	2016	2011	2016	2016
Total services	**1 242**	**1 436**	**-1.1**	**1 525**	**1 818**	**-0.6**
Goods-related services	47	48	2.6	31	31	-2.4
Transport	289	298	-5.3	529	480	-5.6
Travel	404	477	0.3	335	573	2.1
Other services	501	613	-0.3	630	733	0.9

Developing economies: Africa

Service category	Exports			Imports		
	Value		Annual growth rate	Value		Annual growth rate
	(Billions of US$)		(Percentage)	(Billions of US$)		(Percentage)
	2011	2016	2016	2011	2016	2016
Total services	**98**	**96**	**-5.6**	**171**	**144**	**-10.1**
Goods-related services	2	2	8.8	0	1	15.5
Transport	26	26	-8.6	61	55	-9.7
Travel	42	35	-7.7	28	21	-17.7
Other services	28	32	-1.2	83	68	-8.1

Developing economies: America

Service category	Exports			Imports		
	Value		Annual growth rate	Value		Annual growth rate
	(Billions of US$)		(Percentage)	(Billions of US$)		(Percentage)
	2011	2016	2016	2011	2016	2016
Total services	**154**	**171**	**0.7**	**210**	**203**	**-4.0**
Goods-related services	4	4	0.9	0	1	-3.0
Transport	30	27	-3.8	66	56	-5.9
Travel	60	79	5.5	49	51	-1.6
Other services	60	60	-3.0	93	95	-4.2

Developing economies: Asia and Oceania

Service category	Exports			Imports		
	Value		Annual growth rate	Value		Annual growth rate
	(Billions of US$)		(Percentage)	(Billions of US$)		(Percentage)
	2011	2016	2016	2011	2016	2016
Total services	**989**	**1 169**	**-1.0**	**1 144**	**1 471**	**1.0**
Goods-related services	42	42	2.5	30	30	-2.8
Transport	232	244	-5.1	402	370	-4.9
Travel	302	362	0.1	258	500	3.5
Other services	413	520	0.1	454	571	3.1

Transition economies

Service category	Exports			Imports		
	Value (Billions of US$)		Annual growth rate (Percentage)	Value (Billions of US$)		Annual growth rate (Percentage)
	2011	2016	2016	2011	2016	2016
Total services	**116**	**107**	**-0.9**	**143**	**126**	**-11.0**
Goods-related services	9	7	11.9	2	3	8.7
Transport	40	37	-1.9	30	23	-2.2
Travel	27	24	1.6	47	40	-21.1
Other services	40	39	-3.5	65	61	-7.0

Developed economies

Service category	Exports			Imports		
	Value (Billions of US$)		Annual growth rate (Percentage)	Value (Billions of US$)		Annual growth rate (Percentage)
	2011	2016	2016	2011	2016	2016
Total services	**3 048**	**3 337**	**1.0**	**2 613**	**2 853**	**2.3**
Goods-related services	97	112	2.5	55	75	1.2
Transport	575	518	-3.9	555	521	-1.9
Travel	636	704	2.8	573	586	4.7
Other services	1 741	2 003	1.7	1 430	1 671	3.0

Table 2.2.2 | **Developing economies' exports of selected services by region, 2016**
(Millions of United States dollars)

Group of economies	Insurance and pension services	Financial services	Charges for the use of intellectual property n.i.e.	Telecommunications, computer, and information services	Other business services
Developing Africa	**1 540**	**2 260**	**260**	**5 960**	**14 150**
Eastern Africa	320	350	90	1 140	1 580
Middle Africa	-	-	-	-	-
Northern Africa	590	650	30	2 830	4 100
Southern Africa	200	810	110	600	2 430
Western Africa	160	380	-	1 180	5 390
Developing America	**5 260**	**3 100**	**1 350**	**7 800**	**34 780**
Caribbean	-	-	70	540	5 740
Central America	3 040	1 370	240	2 440	3 790
South America	1 750	1 220	1 040	4 820	25 260
Developing Asia and Oceania	**20 610**	**59 050**	**17 670**	**119 690**	**241 600**
Eastern Asia	6 530	26 800	9 680	34 300	100 910
Southern Asia	2 470	5 670	560	58 240	55 410
South-Eastern Asia	7 000	20 930	5 660	16 280	75 900
Western Asia	4 610	5 650	1 770	10 870	9 380
Oceania	-	-	-	-	-

Economic trends

KEY FIGURES **2016**

World real
GDP growth

+2.2%

Developing
economies' current
account balance

+US$169 billion

FDI inflows to LDCs

US$38 billion

Change in
free-market
commodity prices

+3.5%

3.1 Gross domestic product

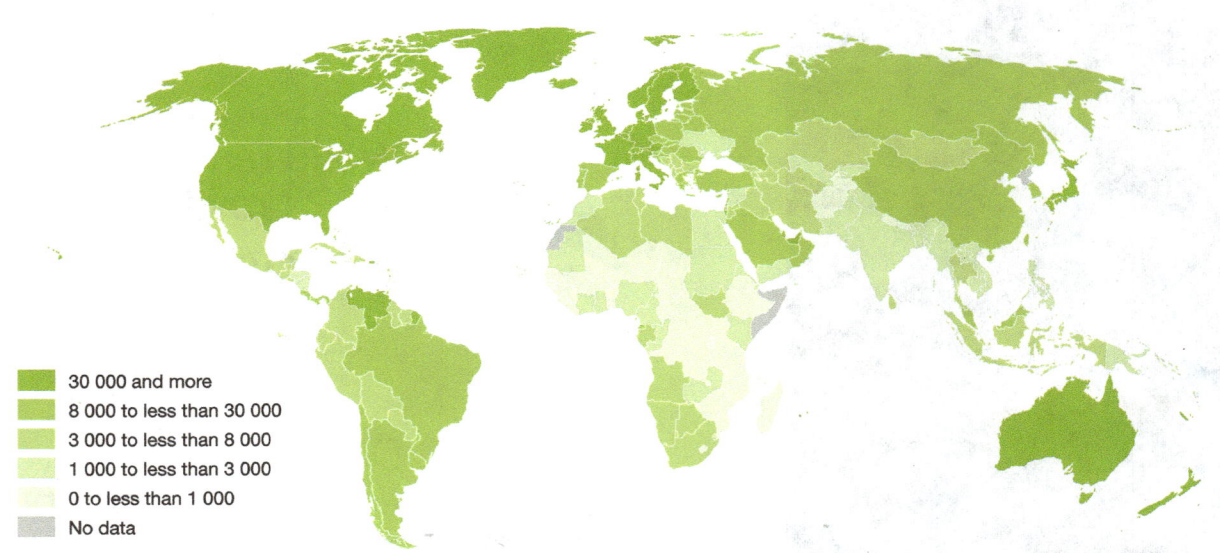

- 30 000 and more
- 8 000 to less than 30 000
- 3 000 to less than 8 000
- 1 000 to less than 3 000
- 0 to less than 1 000
- No data

Concepts and definitions

GDP is an aggregate measure of production, income and expenditure of an economy. As production measure, it represents the gross value added, i.e. the output net of intermediate consumption, achieved by all resident units engaged in production, plus any taxes less subsidies on products not included in the value of output. As income measure, it represents the sum of primary incomes (gross wages and entrepreneurial income) distributed by resident producers, plus taxes and less subsidies on production and imports. As expenditure measure, it represents the sum of expenditure on final consumption, gross capital formation (i.e. investment) and exports after deduction of imports (United Nations et al., 2009).

The GDP figures presented in this section are calculated from the expenditure side.

Gross domestic product growth remaining sluggish

In 2016, world GDP growth remained slow. Since 2011, it has grown at an average annual rate of 2.4 per cent, much lower than the average of 3.3 per cent in the decade prior to the financial crisis. In 2016, the growth rate of world GDP dropped to 2.2 per cent, falling back to 2012 levels.

Large differences in GDP per capita persist throughout the world. In 2016, most developed economies produced an output per person greater than US$30 000, with the main exceptions in Eastern Europe. By contrast, many developing economies in Western and Eastern Africa and in South-Eastern Asia, primarily least developed economies, had less than US$1 000 per person to spend. Developing economies in America, Northern and Southern Africa and in Western and Eastern Asia mostly achieved output levels above US$3 000 per capita.

Figure 3.1.1 | **World real gross domestic product annual growth rate**
(Percentage)

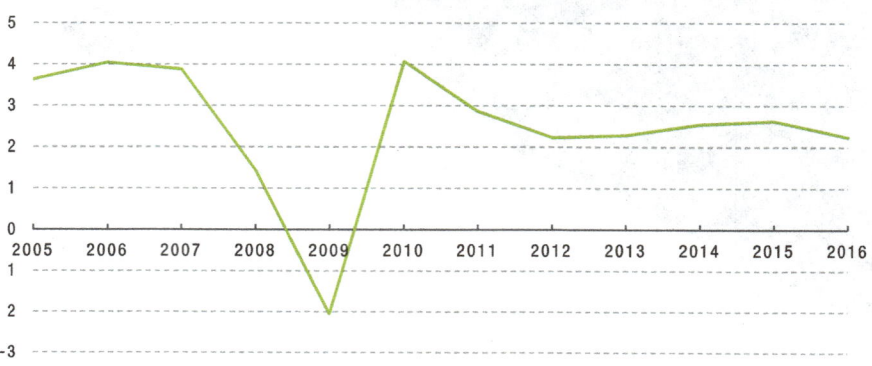

Note: At constant 2005 United States dollars.

Disparities in growth across groups of economies

In 2016, developing economies grew by 3.7 per cent. However, there were considerable regional variations. In developing America economic output contracted slightly, while developing Asia and Oceania achieved GDP growth of 5 per cent. GDP growth in LDCs was 4 per cent – well below the 2030 Agenda for Sustainable Development target of 7 per cent growth.

GDP in transition economies remained almost constant. Developed economies increased their output by a moderate 1.6 per cent – the same annual rate as the last five years on average.

Figure 3.1.2 | **Growth of real gross domestic product by group of economies, 2016** (Percentage)

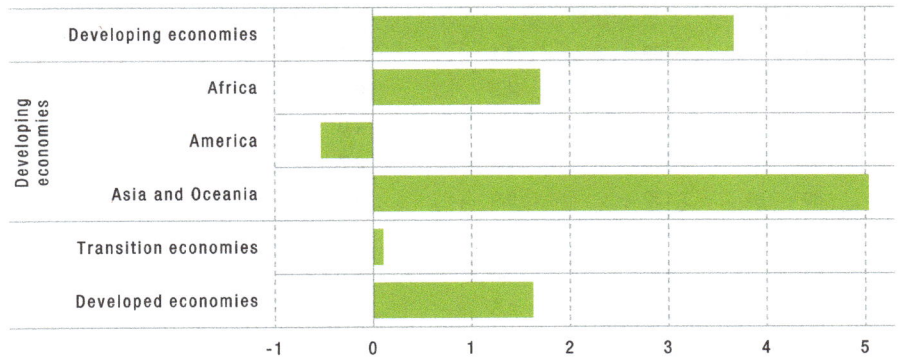

Note: At constant 2005 United States dollars.

World inequality decreasing

Over the last 10 years, the global distribution of GDP per capita has become more equal. For example, in 2006, the poorest economies accounting for 80 per cent of the world's population contributed 20 per cent to world GDP. By 2016, their share in GDP rose to 32 per cent. Between 2011 and 2016, however, inequalities in GDP per capita reduced mainly among economies with moderately high income. The relative distance between the richest and poorest economies in the world remained almost unchanged.

Figure 3.1.3 | **Distribution of world gross domestic product, 2016** (Percentage)

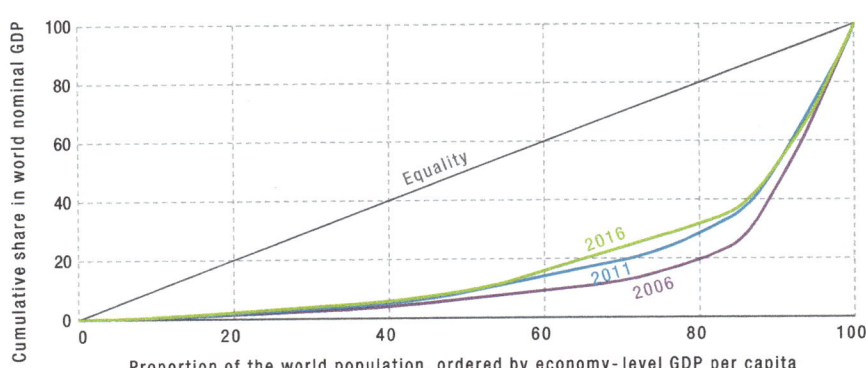

Note: Lorenz curves, as in this graph, reveal the structure of inequality. Inequality is greater the further the curve runs below the diagonal line (see annex 6.3). Inequality within economies is not considered.

World GDP still growing slowly: **2.2%**

Growth in LDCs' GDP (4.0%) remains **below** the **2030 Agenda** target of **7%**

Output in transition economies stagnant

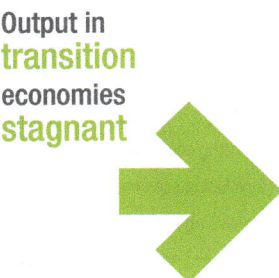

The richest 20 per cent account for **two thirds** of **world GDP**

Table 3.1.1 | **Gross domestic product and gross domestic product per capita**

Group of economies	Value		Annual growth rate			
	Nominal GDP	Nominal GDP per capita	Real GDP[a]		Real GDP[a] per capita	
	(Billions of US$)	(US$)	(Percentage)		(Percentage)	
	2016	2016	2011-2016	2016	2011-2016	2016
World	**76 349**	**10 227**	**2.4**	**2.2**	**1.2**	**1.1**
Developing economies	30 243	4 952	4.3	3.7	2.9	2.3
Developing economies: Africa	2 238	1 829	3.3	1.7	0.6	-0.9
Developing economies: America	5 870	9 256	1.0	-0.5	-0.1	-1.6
Developing economies: Asia and Oceania	22 136	5 208	5.4	5.0	4.3	4.0
Transition economies	1 872	6 113	0.5	0.1	0.2	-0.2
Developed economies	44 234	42 063	1.6	1.6	1.3	1.3
Selected groups						
Developing economies excluding China	18 861	4 009	3.1	2.4	1.4	0.8
Developing economies excluding LDCs	29 202	5 696	4.3	3.7	3.1	2.5
LDCs	1 041	1 061	4.8	4.0	2.3	1.6
LLDCs	733	1 489	5.5	2.7	2.6	0.4
SIDS (UNCTAD)	89	7 132	0.9	0.3	-0.2	-0.7
HIPCs (IMF)	551	803	5.9	4.5	3.0	1.7
BRICS	17 004	5 423	5.2	4.7	4.3	3.9
G20	59 002	13 057	2.5	2.2	1.6	1.5

[a] At constant 2005 United States dollars.

Table 3.1.2 | **Nominal gross domestic product by type of expenditure, 2015**
(Percentage)

Group of economies	Final consumption		Gross capital formation	Net exports of goods and services
	Households[a]	Government[b]		
World	**57.6**	**16.4**	**25.6**	**0.4**
Developing economies	52.4	14.4	33.0	0.3
Developing economies: Africa	68.7	14.7	23.2	-6.9
Developing economies: America	69.0	16.6	21.8	-7.1
Developing economies: Asia and Oceania	46.6	13.8	36.8	2.9
Transition economies	55.3	17.6	21.3	5.4
Developed economies	61.2	17.7	20.9	0.2
Selected groups				
Developing economies excluding China	61.3	14.8	25.4	-1.6
Developing economies excluding LDCs	51.8	14.5	33.2	0.7
LDCs	69.3	11.5	26.2	-9.8
LLDCs	60.7	13.4	28.9	-4.9
SIDS (UNCTAD)	64.6	17.4	17.3	0.5
HIPCs (IMF)	70.5	14.0	26.6	-12.2
BRICS	45.2	14.5	38.0	2.4
G20	57.4	16.3	26.2	0.1

[a] Households including non-profit institutions serving households.
[b] General government.

Table 3.1.3 | **Nominal gross value added by economic activity**
(Percentage)

Group of economies	Year	Agriculture	Industry	Services
World	**2005**	**3.3**	**28.6**	**68.0**
	2015	**4.4**	**28.4**	**67.2**
Developing economies	2005	9.2	39.0	51.7
	2015	9.0	36.2	54.8
Developing economies: Africa	2005	14.8	35.2	50.0
	2015	16.0	30.0	54.0
Developing economies: America	2005	5.4	34.8	59.8
	2015	5.4	29.9	64.7
Developing economies: Asia and Oceania	2005	9.7	41.1	49.1
	2015	9.1	38.2	52.7
Transition economies	2005	7.0	37.5	55.6
	2015	6.5	32.5	61.0
Developed economies	2005	1.4	25.1	73.5
	2015	1.3	23.0	75.7
Selected groups				
Developing economies excluding China	2005	8.5	36.8	54.7
	2015	8.9	32.9	58.2
Developing economies excluding LDCs	2005	8.7	39.3	51.9
	2015	8.6	36.3	55.1
LDCs	2005	24.7	30.7	44.6
	2015	21.7	31.2	47.1
LLDCs	2005	19.9	33.1	47.0
	2015	16.4	31.5	52.1
SIDS (UNCTAD)	2005	6.8	32.2	61.0
	2015	7.6	27.9	64.5
HIPCs (IMF)	2005	26.7	25.8	47.5
	2015	25.0	26.9	48.2
BRICS	2005	10.7	39.9	49.5
	2015	9.3	37.1	53.6
G20	2005	2.8	27.6	69.6
	2015	3.9	27.9	68.2

Table 3.1.4 | **World gross domestic product by quintile**

World population quintile[b]	GDP per capita			Share in world nominal GDP
	Nominal value	Real annual growth rate[a]		
	(US$)	(Percentage)		(Percentage)
	2016	2011-2016	2016	2016
1st quintile	1 088	3.1	3.2	2.1
2nd quintile	1 844	4.4	4.2	3.6
3rd quintile	5 063	1.9	2.0	9.9
4th quintile	8 204	4.5	3.9	16.0
5th quintile	34 935	1.1	1.0	68.3
TOTAL	**10 227**	**1.1**	**1.1**	**100.0**

[a] At constant 2005 United States dollars.
[b] With respect to nominal GDP per capita in 2016, assigned in equal amount to people within economies.

3.2 Current account

Map 3.2 | **Current account balance as a ratio to gross domestic product, 2016**
| (Percentage)

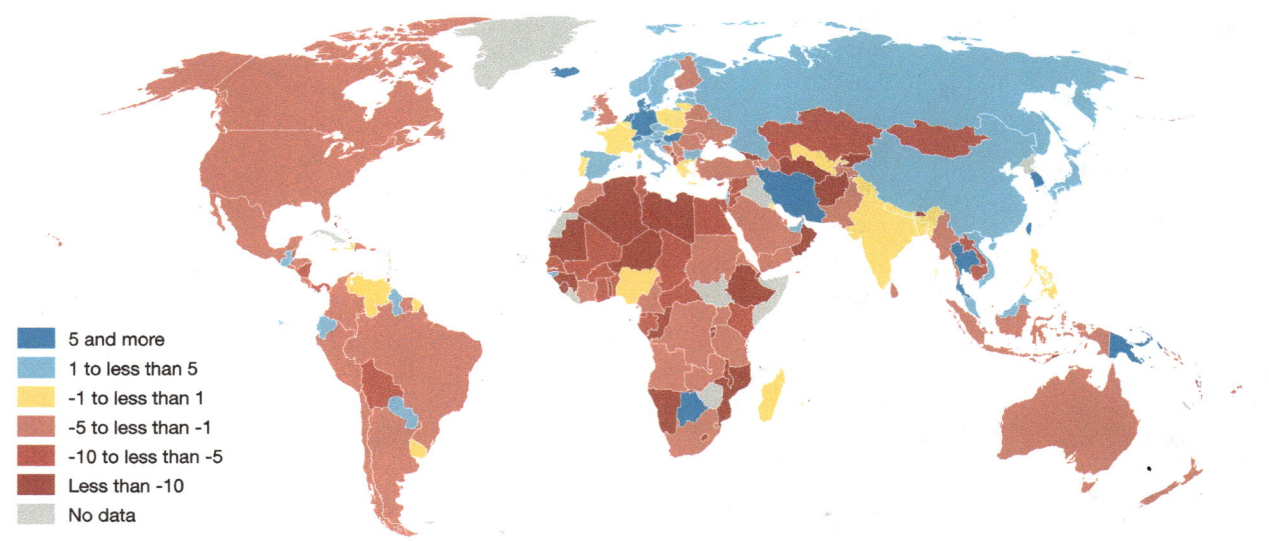

- 5 and more
- 1 to less than 5
- -1 to less than 1
- -5 to less than -1
- -10 to less than -5
- Less than -10
- No data

Concepts and definitions

The current account, within the balance of payments, displays the transactions between residents and non-residents of a reporting economy, involving economic values, namely the cross-national exchange of goods and services as well as cross-national transfers of primary and secondary income.

The current account balance shows the difference between the sum of exports and income receivable and the sum of imports and income payable, where exports and imports refer to both goods and services, while income refers to both primary and secondary income. A surplus in the current account is recorded when receipts exceed expenditures; a deficit is recorded when expenditures exceed receipts.

The current account data in this subchapter correspond to the latest reporting standard, known as BPM6, defined by the International Monetary Fund (2009).

Geographic distribution of current account imbalances

The receipts that economies obtain from transactions with other economies are often significantly different from their payments made. In 2016, higher receipts than payments, as reflected by a positive current account balance, were recorded for several economies in Europe and Eastern Asia. Most economies in America, Africa, Western Asia and Oceania ran current account deficits. Libya and Mozambique reached deficits as high as 40 and 36 per cent of GDP, respectively.

Figure 3.2.1 | **Balances in the current account**
| (Billions of United States dollars)

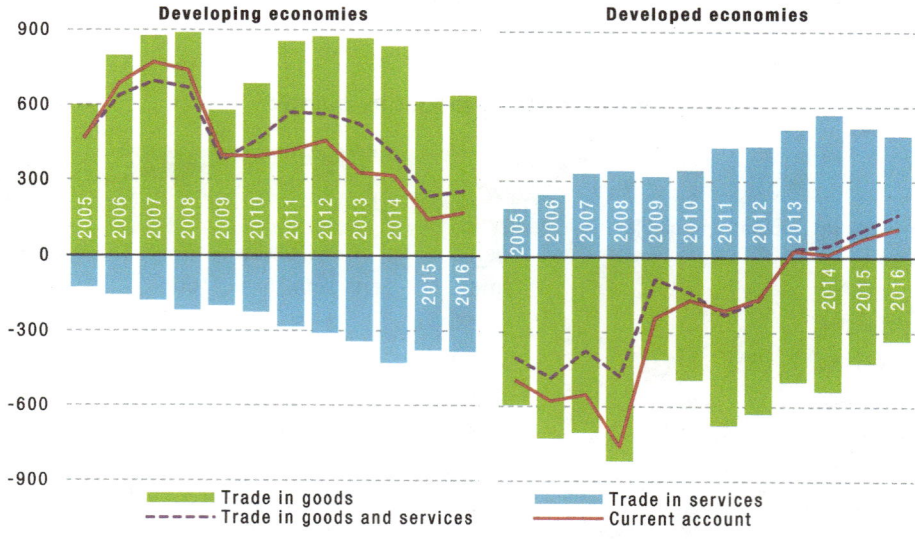

- Trade in goods
- - - Trade in goods and services
- Trade in services
- Current account

Note: Current account deficits and surpluses do not add up to zero at the world level, due to imperfect geographic coverage and cross-country differences in compilation methods.

Recent developments

In 2016, the aggregate current account surplus for developing economies increased slightly to US$169 billion (0.6 per cent of GDP), from US$143 billion, after falling during the three previous years. This slight increase was largely due to a moderate growth in the surplus in the goods account that outweighed increases in the deficit in the services account.

The current account for developed economies had been in deficit for several years but in balance during 2013 and 2014. Since then, a slight surplus has emerged, amounting to US$113 billion (0.3 per cent of GDP) in 2016. The recent growth in the current account surplus has been driven by a considerable reduction in the deficit in the goods account, while the surplus in the services account has decreased at a slower pace.

Figure 3.2.2 | **Balances in least developed countries' current accounts**
(Billions of United States dollars)

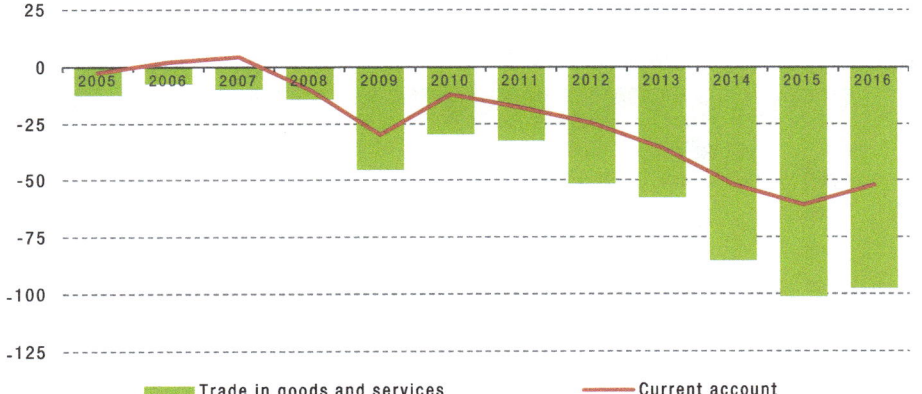

Trade in goods and services ———— Current account

Recovery in least developed countries

The reversal of trend in 2016, as outlined above for the developing economies as a whole, can also be seen in the current accounts of LDCs. After five years of continuous decline, their balance improved in 2016, leading to a reduction in the deficit from US$61 billion to US$52 billion. The trade deficit reduced from US$101 billion to US$98 billion.

Accounting for 5 per cent of GDP, the LDCs' current account deficit is still high compared to other developing economies. Higher relative deficits were registered for landlocked developing countries (LLDCs) (6 per cent), small-island developing States (SIDS) (8 per cent) and heavily indebted poor countries (HIPC) (8 per cent).

Some African economies had current account deficits of up to 40 per cent of GDP in 2016

The surplus of developing economies has stopped shrinking

The surplus of developed economies has grown to

US$ 113 billion

LDCs' deficit reduced by 15 per cent

Table 3.2.1 | Current account balance by group of economies

Group of economies	Value (Billions of US$)			Ratio to GDP (Percentage)		
	2011-2016	2015	2016	2011-2016	2015	2016
World[a]	**322**	**264**	**277**	**0.4**	**0.4**	**0.4**
Developing economies	304	143	169	1.1	0.5	0.6
Developing economies: Africa	-83	-162	-129	-3.6	-7.2	-6.0
Developing economies: America	-143	-171	-97	-2.4	-3.2	-1.7
Developing economies: Asia and Oceania	531	476	395	2.7	2.2	1.8
Transition economies	43	48	-5	1.6	2.5	-0.3
Developed economies	-26	73	113	-0.1	0.2	0.3
Selected groups						
Developing economies excluding China	98	-161	-27	0.5	-0.9	-0.1
Developing economies excluding LDCs	345	204	221	1.3	0.7	0.8
LDCs	-41	-61	-52	-4.5	-6.7	-5.4
LLDCs	-17	-37	-43	-2.4	-5.2	-6.4
SIDS (UNCTAD)	-2	-3	-7	-1.9	-3.3	-8.2
HIPCs (IMF)	-43	-48	-46	-8.2	-9.1	-8.3
BRICS	136	277	177	0.8	1.7	1.0
G20	-88	7	11	-0.2	0.0	0.0

[a] Current account deficits and surpluses do not add up to zero at the world level, due to imperfect geographic coverage and cross-country differences in compilation methods.

Table 3.2.2 | Current account balance in largest surplus and deficit economies

Economy (Ranked by 2016 value)	2011-2016 Value (Billions of US$)	2011-2016 Ratio to GDP (Percentage)	2015 Value (Billions of US$)	2015 Ratio to GDP (Percentage)	2016 Value (Billions of US$)	2016 Ratio to GDP (Percentage)
Germany	266	7.4	288	8.6	289	8.4
China	206	2.1	304	2.7	196	1.7
Japan	99	1.9	134	3.1	187	3.8
Korea, Republic of	73	5.4	106	7.7	99	7.1
China, Taiwan Province of	57	11.1	75	14.4	72	13.7
⋮	⋮	⋮	⋮	⋮	⋮	⋮
Turkey	-49	-6.3	-32	-4.5	-33	-4.6
Australia	-48	-3.4	-58	-4.7	-33	-2.6
Canada	-54	-3.1	-53	-3.4	-51	-3.3
United Kingdom	-107	-3.9	-123	-4.3	-116	-4.5
United States	-413	-2.4	-435	-2.4	-452	-2.4

Table 3.2.3 | Current accounts of leading exporters (goods and services) by group of economies, 2016

Developing economies: Africa

Economy (Ranked by export share)	Current account balance Value (Billions of US$)	Current account balance Ratio to GDP (Percentage)	Trade balance[a] Value (Billions of US$)	Exports[a] Share in world (Percentage)	Imports[a] Share in world (Percentage)
South Africa	-9	-3.2	1	0.4	0.4
Nigeria	3	0.6	(e) -9	(e) 0.2	(e) 0.2
Egypt	-20	-7.1	(e) -39	(e) 0.2	(e) 0.4
Morocco	-5	-4.4	-11	0.2	0.2
Algeria	-26	-15.9	(e) -26	(e) 0.2	(e) 0.3
Developing Africa	**-129**	**-6.0**	**-167**	**2.2**	**3.1**

[a] Goods and services

Developing economies: America

Economy (Ranked by export share)	Current account balance		Trade balance[a]	Exports[a]	Imports[a]
	Value	Ratio to GDP	Value	Share in world	Share in world
	(Billions of US$)	(Percentage)	(Billions of US$)	(Percentage)	(Percentage)
Mexico	-22	-2.2	-21	1.9	2.1
Brazil	-24	-1.3	(e) 15	(e) 1.1	(e) 1.0
Argentina	-15	-2.7	(e) -3	(e) 0.3	(e) 0.4
Chile	-4	-1.5	(e) 2	(e) 0.3	(e) 0.3
Peru	-5	-2.7	(e) 0	(e) 0.2	(e) 0.2
Developing America	**-97**	**-1.7**	**-46**	**5.2**	**5.5**

[a] Goods and services

Developing economies: Asia and Oceania

Economy (Ranked by export share)	Current account balance		Trade balance[a]	Exports[a]	Imports[a]
	Value	Ratio to GDP	Value	Share in world	Share in world
	(Billions of US$)	(Percentage)	(Billions of US$)	(Percentage)	(Percentage)
China	196	1.7	250	10.6	9.7
Korea, Republic of	99	7.1	103	2.9	2.5
China, Hong Kong SAR	15	4.6	(e) 6	(e) 2.9	(e) 2.9
Singapore	57	19.1	77	2.5	2.2
India	-12	-0.5	(e) -79	(e) 2.1	(e) 2.5
Developing Asia and Oceania	**395**	**1.8**	**467**	**33.4**	**31.9**

[a] Goods and services

Transition economies

Economy (Ranked by export share)	Current account balance		Trade balance[a]	Exports[a]	Imports[a]
	Value	Ratio to GDP	Value	Share in world	Share in world
	(Billions of US$)	(Percentage)	(Billions of US$)	(Percentage)	(Percentage)
Russian Federation	26	2.0	66	1.6	1.3
Ukraine	-4	-4.2	(e) -6	(e) 0.2	(e) 0.3
Kazakhstan	-9	-6.3	(e) 5	(e) 0.2	(e) 0.2
Belarus	-2	-2.1	0	0.1	0.1
Serbia	-2	-3.4	(e) -2	(e) 0.1	(e) 0.1
Transition economies	**-5**	**-0.3**	**47**	**2.6**	**2.5**

[a] Goods and services

Developed economies

Economy (Ranked by export share)	Current account balance		Trade balance[a]	Exports[a]	Imports[a]
	Value	Ratio to GDP	Value	Share in world	Share in world
	(Billions of US$)	(Percentage)	(Billions of US$)	(Percentage)	(Percentage)
United States	-452	-2.4	(e) -501	(e) 10.7	(e) 13.4
Germany	289	8.4	(e) 261	(e) 7.7	(e) 6.6
Japan	187	3.8	40	3.9	3.8
France	-23	-0.9	(e) -29	(e) 3.6	(e) 3.8
United Kingdom	-116	-4.5	(e) -52	(e) 3.6	(e) 3.9
Developed economies	**113**	**0.3**	**169**	**56.6**	**57.0**

[a] Goods and services

3.3 Foreign direct investment

Map 3.3 | **Foreign direct investment inflows, 2016**
(Percentage of gross domestic product)

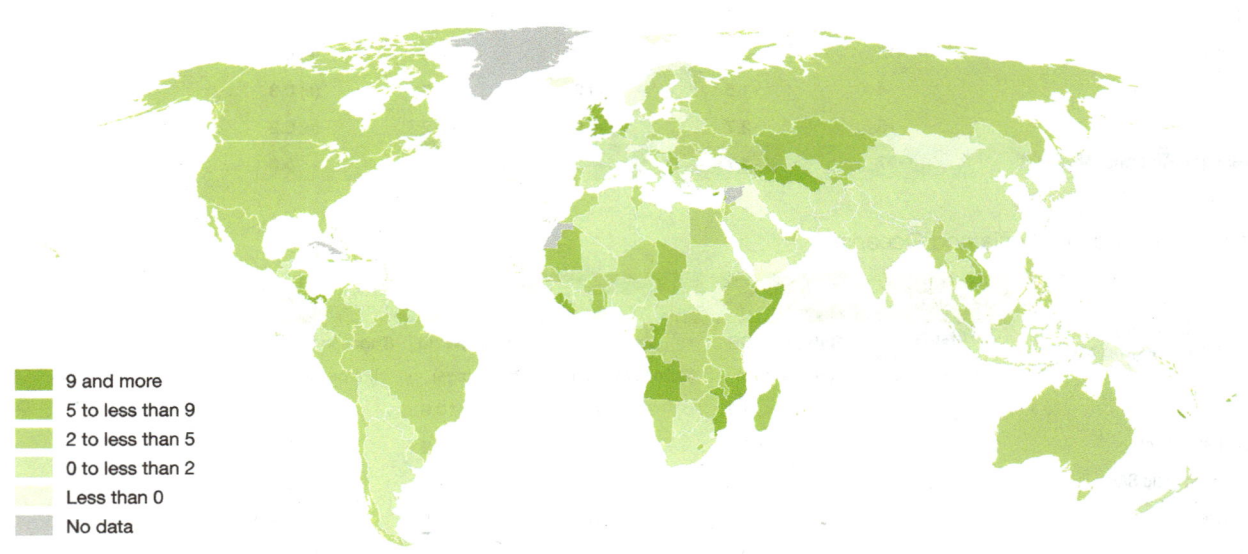

- 9 and more
- 5 to less than 9
- 2 to less than 5
- 0 to less than 2
- Less than 0
- No data

Concepts and definitions

Foreign direct investment (FDI) is defined as an investment reflecting a lasting interest and control by a foreign direct investor, resident in one economy, in an enterprise resident in another economy (foreign affiliate).

FDI inflows comprise capital provided by a foreign direct investor to a foreign affiliate, or capital received by a foreign direct investor from a foreign affiliate. FDI outflows represent the same flows from the perspective of the other economy.

FDI flows are presented on a net basis, i.e. as credits less debits. Thus in cases of reverse investment or disinvestment, FDI may be negative.

FDI stock is the value of capital and reserves attributable to a non-resident parent enterprise, plus the net indebtedness of foreign affiliates to parent enterprises (UNCTAD, 2017b).

Trends and global patterns of inflows

In 2016, global FDI inflows fell by 2 per cent to US$1.75 trillion, after a considerable increase of one third, the previous year. FDI inflows in 2016 were particularly low, compared to GDP, in most developing economies and in large parts of Europe. By contrast, several economies in Central America, Middle Africa, Central and South-East Asia as well as in the north-west of Europe received inflows greater than 5 per cent of GDP. In some smaller economies, such as Luxembourg, Hong Kong SAR or Singapore, and especially in a number of small island economies, the ratio of FDI inflows to GDP was very high.

In absolute terms, the largest recipient of FDI in 2016 was the United States of America, where inflows reached US$391 billion, followed by the United Kingdom (US$254 billion) and China (US$134 billion).

Figure 3.3.1 | **World foreign direct investment inflows**
(Billions of United States dollars)

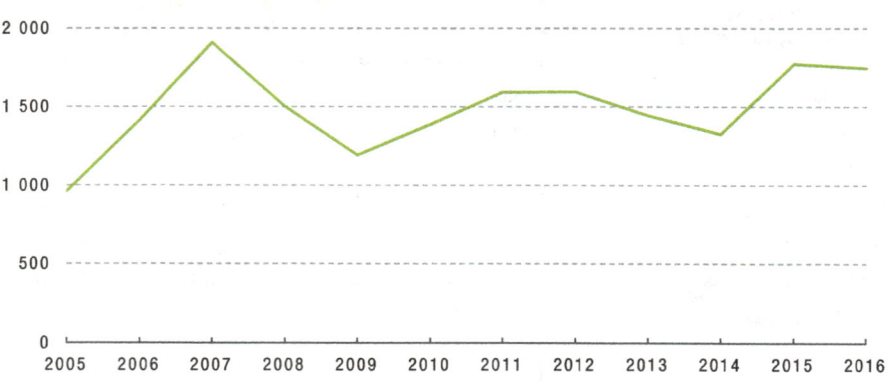

Note: Excluding financial centres in the Caribbean (see the note to table 3.3.1 below).

Inflows and outflows by economic group

In developing economies, total FDI inflows were larger than total FDI outflows, with inflows exceeding outflows by two thirds, more or less the same rate as in 2011. The outflows from American developing economies were negligible in 2016. In transition economies, inflows were almost three times as high as outflows, mainly as a result of a considerable reduction of outflows over recent years. By contrast, for developed economies FDI outflows exceeded inflows.

Figure 3.3.2 | **Foreign direct investment inflows and outflows, 2016**
(Billions of United States dollars)

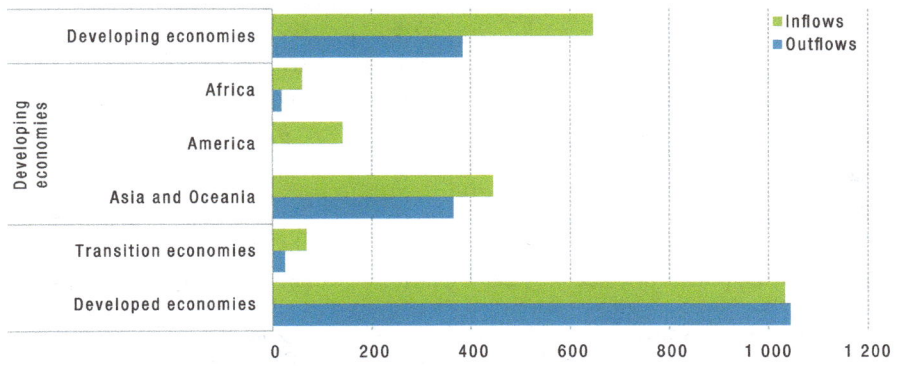

Note: Excluding financial centres in the Caribbean (see note, table 3.3.1).

Origins and destinations of foreign direct investment

In 2016, developing economies attracted one third of global FDI inflows. This share had been over 50 per cent in 2014 but has shrunk over the last two years. In 2016, one quarter of global FDI was directed to developing economies in Asia and Oceania and less than 10 per cent to developing economies in Africa and America, each. Looking at the origins of global FDI, around 70 per cent were initiated by investors from developed economies. Out of these, 35 per cent originated from Europe and 25 per cent from Northern America.[1]

[1] For further analyses on that topic, see UNCTAD (2017b).

Figure 3.3.3 | **Selected foreign direct investment flows**
(Percentage of world total)

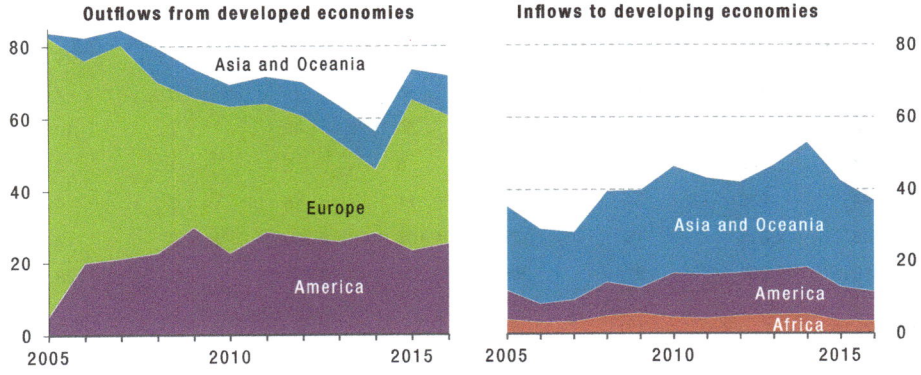

Note: Excluding financial centres in the Caribbean (see note, table 3.3.1).

Global **FDI down** by **2%** in 2016

The **United States of America** was **host** to FDI of **US$391 billion**

Developing economies **received two thirds more** FDI than they initiated

Declining importance of **developing** economies as **FDI targets**

Table 3.3.1 | Foreign direct investment flows by group of economies

Group of economies	Inflows				Outflows			
	Value (Billions of US$)		Ratio to GDP (Percentage)		Value (Billions of US$)		Ratio to GDP (Percentage)	
	2011	2016	2011	2016	2011	2016	2011	2016
World	**1 591**	**1 746**	**2.2**	**2.3**	**1 576**	**1 452**	**2.2**	**1.9**
Developing economies	688	646	2.7	2.1	390	383	1.6	1.3
Developing economies: Africa	66	59	3.1	2.7	23	18	1.2	1.0
Developing economies: America	194	142	3.3	2.5	48	1	0.8	0.0
Developing economies: Asia and Oceania	428	445	2.5	2.0	320	365	1.9	1.7
Transition economies	79	68	2.9	3.6	56	25	2.1	1.4
Developed economies	824	1 032	1.8	2.3	1 130	1 044	2.5	2.4
Selected groups								
Developing economies excluding China	564	512	3.2	2.7	316	200	1.8	1.1
Developing economies excluding LDCs	649	608	2.6	2.1	370	372	1.5	1.3
LDCs	39	38	5.0	3.6	20	12	4.2	2.0
LLDCs	36	24	5.6	3.3	6	-2	1.4	-0.5
SIDS (UNCTAD)	2	2	3.2	3.3	0	0	0.4	-0.3
HIPCs (IMF)	26	23	5.8	4.2	1	1	0.3	0.3
BRICS	297	277	2.1	1.6	147	206	1.0	1.2
G20	897	1 147	1.6	1.9	1 041	851	1.8	1.4

Note: Excluding financial centres in the Caribbean, namely: Anguilla, Antigua and Barbuda, Aruba, Barbados, British Virgin Islands, Cayman Islands, Curaçao, Dominica, Grenada, Montserrat, Saint Kitts and Nevis, Saint Lucia, Saint Vincent and the Grenadines, Sint Maarten, the Bahamas and Turks and Caicos Island.

Table 3.3.2 | Foreign direct investment stock by group of economies

Group of economies	Inward stock				Outward stock			
	Value (Billions of US$)		Ratio to GDP (Percentage)		Value (Billions of US$)		Ratio to GDP (Percentage)	
	2011	2016	2011	2016	2011	2016	2011	2016
World	**20 953**	**26 728**	**29**	**35**	**21 370**	**26 160**	**29**	**35**
Developing economies	6 413	9 078	25	30	3 412	5 809	14	20
Developing economies: Africa	634	837	29	38	151	269	8	14
Developing economies: America	1 640	1 960	28	34	446	569	8	10
Developing economies: Asia and Oceania	4 138	6 281	24	28	2 815	4 970	16	23
Transition economies	688	730	25	39	356	389	13	22
Developed economies	13 850	16 917	31	38	17 602	19 962	39	45
Selected groups								
Developing economies excluding China	5 701	7 723	32	41	2 987	4 528	17	25
Developing economies excluding LDCs	6 225	8 752	25	30	3 394	5 763	14	20
LDCs	188	326	24	33	18	45	3	7
LLDCs	222	330	34	49	36	45	7	10
SIDS (UNCTAD)	37	45	52	64	3	3	4	4
HIPCs (IMF)	144	276	32	50	11	15	3	4
BRICS	2 136	2 815	15	17	1 107	2 106	8	12
G20	11 610	15 282	21	26	13 206	16 712	23	28

Note: Excluding financial centres in the Caribbean (see note, table 3.3.1).

Table 3.3.3 | **Foreign direct investment inflows, top 20 host economies, 2016**

Economy (Ranked by inflow value)	Inflows		Inward stock
	Value	Ratio to GDP	Ratio to GDP
	(Billions of US$)	(Percentage)	(Percentage)
United States	391	2.1	34
United Kingdom	254	9.8	46
China	134	1.2	12
China, Hong Kong SAR	108	33.7	496
Netherlands	92	12.0	105
Singapore	62	20.9	372
British Virgin Islands[a]	59	6 243.3	66 948
Brazil	59	3.3	35
Australia	48	3.8	45
Cayman Islands[a]	45	1 184.2	9 311
India	44	2.0	14
Russian Federation	38	2.9	30
Canada	34	2.2	62
Belgium	33	7.1	101
Italy	29	1.6	19
France	28	1.2	28
Luxembourg	27	46.1	421
Mexico	27	2.6	47
Ireland	22	7.6	286
Sweden	20	3.8	57

[a] Financial centre in the Caribbean

Table 3.3.4 | **Foreign direct investment outflows, top 20 home economies, 2016**

Economy (Ranked by outflow value)	Outflows		Outward stock
	Value	Ratio to GDP	Ratio to GDP
	(Billions of US$)	(Percentage)	(Percentage)
United States	299	1.6	34
China	183	1.6	11
Netherlands	174	22.7	164
Japan	145	3.0	28
British Virgin Islands[a]	95	10 017.3	91 570
Canada	66	4.3	79
China, Hong Kong SAR	62	19.5	477
France	57	2.3	51
Ireland	45	15.2	283
Spain	42	3.4	42
Germany	35	1.0	40
Luxembourg	32	54.3	395
Switzerland	31	4.6	170
Korea, Republic of	27	2.0	22
Russian Federation	27	2.1	26
Cayman Islands[a]	26	677.8	5 398
Singapore	24	8.1	231
Sweden	23	4.5	75
Italy	23	1.2	25
Finland	23	9.7	52

[a] Financial centre in the Caribbean

3.4 Prices

Map 3.4 | **Annual growth of the consumer price index, 2016**
(Percentage)

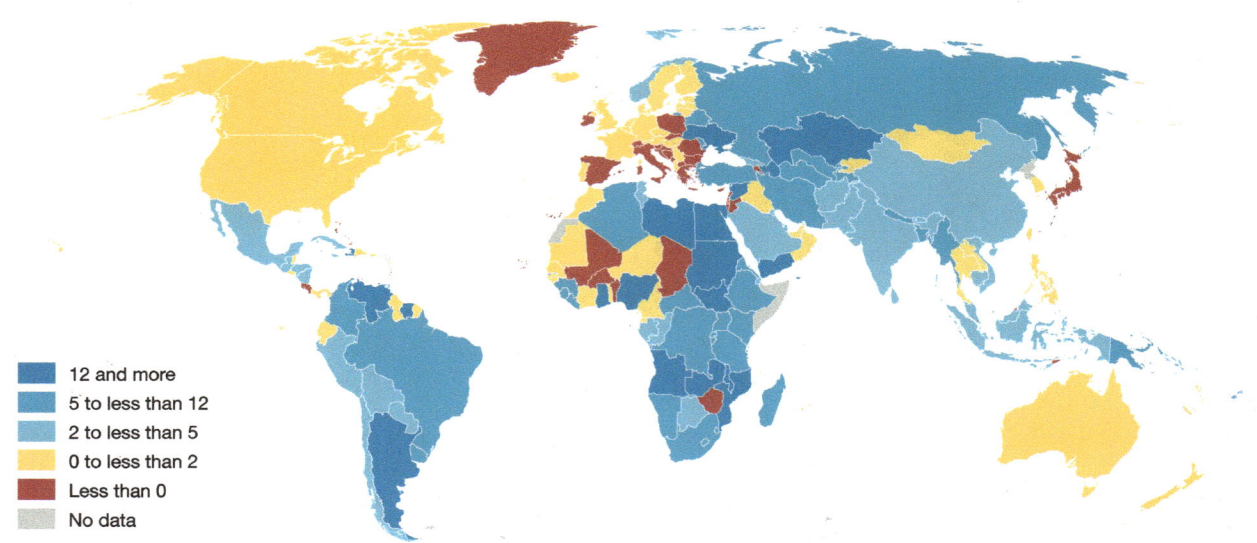

- 12 and more
- 5 to less than 12
- 2 to less than 5
- 0 to less than 2
- Less than 0
- No data

Concepts and definitions

The consumer price index (CPI) measures the price evolution for a basket of consumer goods and services that represents average consumption by private households in an economy.

The UNCTAD commodity price index is a Laspeyres index measuring the price of a bundle of main commodities exported by developing economies relative to the price in the base year 2000. The overall index can be additively decomposed into subindices of individual commodity groups.

The special drawing right is a basket of main currencies (United States dollar, euro, yuan, yen and pound sterling) regularly reviewed by the International Monetary Fund. Thus, changes in the value of the special drawing right result, as a weighted average, from changes in the basket of currencies included.

Consumer prices and exchange rates

Economies that experienced noticeable inflation, as indicated by a growth in consumer prices of greater than 2 per cent, in 2016 comprised primarily transition economies as well as most developing economies in America, Africa (except Western Africa), Southern and Western Asia and Oceania. Inflation rates greater than 12 per cent were recorded for some economies, including Argentina, Kazakhstan, Ukraine, Venezuela and several African economies.

As in the previous year, 2016 was characterized by a depreciation of currencies for most main exporting economies, except Japan, relative to the United States dollar. The exchange rates of the pound sterling (down from 1.53 to 1.35) and the yuan (down from 0.16 to 0.15) to the dollar showed a particularly strong fall, whereas the value of the euro reduced only slightly from US$1.109 to US$1.106.

Figure 3.4.1 | **Exchange rates against the United States dollar**
(Annual average)

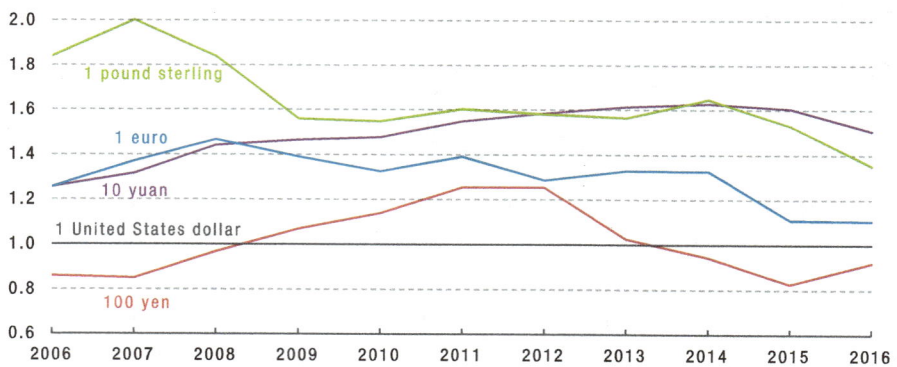

Commodities free-market prices

In 2016, free market prices of the main commodities exported by developing economies showed, on average, a moderate and steady month-on-month growth. As a result, in the second half of the year commodity prices were higher than the previous year, and in December the year-on-year growth rate reached 16 per cent. Thus, 2016 marked a trend reversal after years of decline. This can be expected to have a positive impact on the terms of trade for developing economies with a strong reliance on commodities exports.

Figure 3.4.2 | **Growth in commodity prices, 2016**
(Percentage change of the commodity price index)

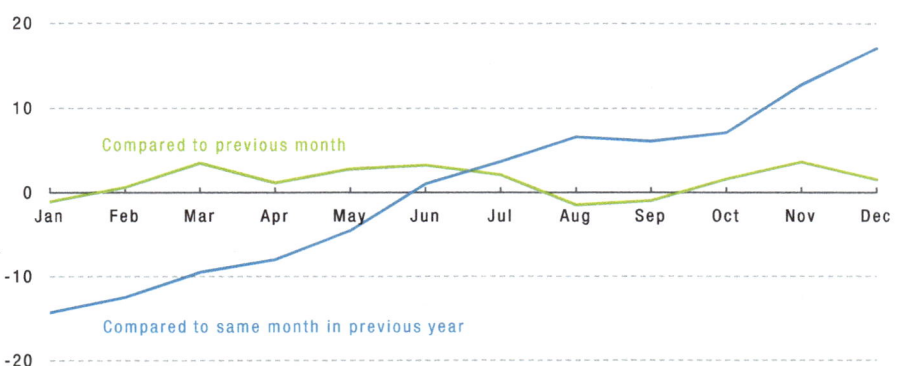

Note: Price index based on special drawing rights.

Prices of the different commodity groups

Price increases across commodity groups were not synchronous. In the first half of 2016, the strongest growth was recorded in the prices of fuels and all food, particularly vegetable oilseeds and oils; in the second half of the year, prices increased mainly for minerals, ores and metals and agricultural raw materials. By contrast, prices for all food steadily fell during the second half of the year, driven by a fall in prices of food other than tropical beverages, vegetable oilseeds and vegetable oils.

Figure 3.4.3 | **Price indices by commodity group, 2016**
(2000=100)

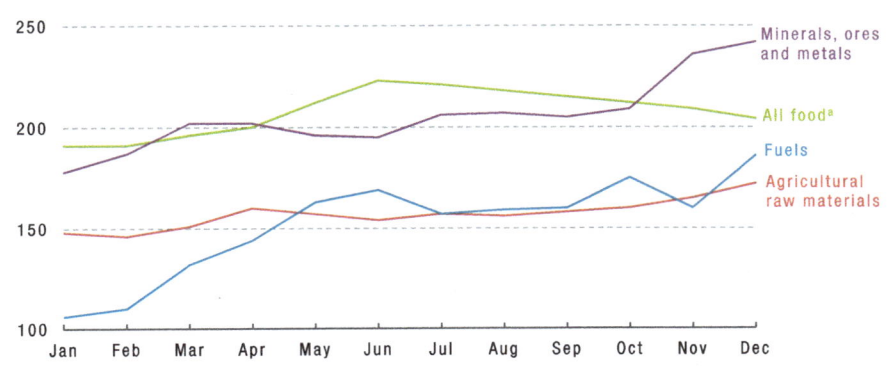

ª All food contains: food in the narrower sense, tropical beverages, vegetable oilseeds and oils.
Note: Price indices based on United States dollars.

Low growth of **consumer prices** in the developed world

Many important exporters' **currencies devalued** further compared with the United States dollar

Commodity prices increased almost continuously over the year

Fuel prices went up by **70%** during the first half of 2016

Table 3.4.1 | Development of consumer prices by group of economies

Group of economies	Consumer price index (2005=100)		Annual growth rate (Percentage)	
	2011	2016	2011-2016	2016
World	**121**	**139**	**2.8**	**3.4**
Developing economies	140	189	6.1	8.5
Developing economies: Africa	158	233	8.1	11.8
Developing economies: America	148	272	13.0	28.0
Developing economies: Asia and Oceania	136	164	3.8	2.9
Transition economies	180	276	8.9	8.0
Developed economies	113	119	1.1	0.7
Selected groups				
Developing economies excluding China	147	212	7.7	11.3
Developing economies excluding LDCs	139	186	5.9	8.3
LDCs	178	288	10.1	15.6
LLDCs	169	253	8.3	14.8
SIDS (UNCTAD)	152	183	3.7	1.5
HIPCs (IMF)	161	217	6.1	6.1
BRICS	138	172	4.4	3.9
G20	118	132	2.2	1.9

Table 3.4.2 | Exchange rate and consumer prices among main exporting economies

Economy (Ranked by share in world exports)	Exchange rate to United States dollar			Consumer price index (2005=100)			Share in world exports[a] (Percentage)
	2014	2015	2016	2014	2015	2016	2016
United States	1.00000	1.00000	1.00000	121	121	123	(e) 10.7
China	0.16278	0.16058	0.15050	131	133	135	10.6
Germany	1.32673	1.10907	1.10615	115	116	116	(e) 7.7
Japan	0.00944	0.00826	0.00919	102	103	103	3.9
France	1.32673	1.10907	1.10615	116	116	116	(e) 3.6
United Kingdom	1.64547	1.52778	1.35019	128	128	129	(e) 3.6
Netherlands	1.32673	1.10907	1.10615	117	118	118	(e) 3.2
Korea, Republic of	0.00095	0.00088	0.00086	127	127	129	2.9
China, Hong Kong SAR	0.12896	0.12900	0.12883	133	137	141	(e) 2.9
Italy	1.32673	1.10907	1.10615	118	118	118	(e) 2.7
Singapore	0.78923	0.72736	0.72382	129	129	128	2.5
Canada	0.90408	0.78180	0.75449	117	118	120	(e) 2.3
Switzerland	1.09152	1.03909	1.01498	104	103	102	2.1
India	0.01639	0.01559	0.01488	214	224	235	(e) 2.1
Spain	1.32673	1.10907	1.10615	120	120	119	(e) 2.0
Mexico	0.07523	0.06310	0.05358	144	148	153	1.9
Belgium	1.32673	1.10907	1.10615	119	120	123	(e) 1.9
United Arab Emirates	0.27229	0.27229	0.27229	105	109	111	1.8
Ireland	1.32673	1.10907	1.10615	113	112	112	(e) 1.7
China, Taiwan Province of	0.03293	0.03134	0.03094	112	112	113	1.7

[a] Exports of goods and services

Table 3.4.3 | **Indices of free-market prices of selected primary commodities**
(2000=100)

Commodity	2010	2011	2012	2013	2014	2015	2016
All commodities	**256**	**302**	**277**	**258**	**243**	**202**	**200**
Food	230	265	270	255	240	204	207
Wheat (US, Hard Red Winter n° 2, FOB Gulf)	204	276	275	270	254	195	165
Maize (US, n° 3 yellow, FOB Gulf)	217	325	334	294	228	195	187
Rice (Thailand, white milled, 5% broken, FOB Bangkok)	256	271	285	255	209	187	191
Sugar (Caribbean ports, FOB bulk basis, I.S.A.)	260	318	263	216	208	164	221
Beef (Australia/New Zealand, US import price FOB port of entry)	174	209	214	209	255	228	203
Bananas, US importer's price, FOB US ports	210	233	235	221	222	229	239
Pepper (Indonesia, white Muntok, FAQ, ex-works Rotterdam)	139	219	226	226	291	333	276
Soybean meal (Hamburg, 44/45° protein, FOB ex-mill)	196	201	255	269	255	187	177
Fish meal (in bulk, 64/65% protein, free carrier price Bremen)	409	372	377	423	416	377	364
Tropical beverages	213	270	212	174	214	197	190
Coffee (Colombian mild Arabicas, ex-dock US)	218	277	199	145	193	146	152
Cocoa beans (Average daily prices New York/London)	353	336	269	275	345	353	326
Tea (Kenya, Best Pekoe Fannings 1, Mombasa auction prices)	125	140	141	107	96	137	116
Vegetables oil seeds and oils	262	333	307	269	253	203	226
Soybeans (US, n° 2 yellow, CIF Rotterdam)	212	255	279	257	232	184	191
Soybean oil (The Netherlands, FOB ex-mill)	297	384	363	313	269	224	239
Sunflower oil (In bulk, European Union, FOB N.W. European ports)	274	347	322	287	230	216	215
Groundnut oil (In bulk, any origin, CIF Rotterdam)	197	264	340	248	184	187	211
Copra (In bulk, Philippines/Indonesia, CIF N.W. European ports)	246	380	243	206	280	241	322
Coconut oil (In bulk, Philippines/Indonesia, CIF Rotterdam)	249	384	247	209	284	246	328
Palm kernel oil (In bulk, Malaysia/Indonesia, CIF Rotterdam)	267	372	250	202	253	205	291
Palm oil (Malaysia/Indonesia, 5% FFA, CIF N.W. European ports)	290	363	322	276	265	201	226
Agricultural raw materials	226	289	223	206	186	161	157
Linseed oil (In bulk, any origin, ex-tank, Rotterdam)	292	358	315	305	305	267	203
Tobacco (Unmanufactured, US import unit value)	144	150	144	153	167	164	160
Cotton (Cotlook A Index, Midd. 1-3/32", CFR Far Eastern)	175	258	150	153	139	119	125
Fine wool, 19 micron, Australia	140	223	183	163	146	137	152
Sisal (Tanzania/Kenya, n° 3 & UG, FOB)	161	210	236	222	254	320	339
Hide (US Chicago packer's heavy native steers, FOB shipping point)	90	102	104	118	138	109	89
Tropical logs, Sapele (Cameroon, high quality, > 80 centimeter, FOB)	175	199	185	190	190	159	158
Rubber (Technically specified rubber 20, New York CIF)	492	660	470	378	270	222	211
Minerals, ores and metals	327	375	322	306	280	218	205
Phosphate rock (Khouribga, 70% BPL, contract, FAS Casablanca)	281	423	425	339	252	269	253
Manganese ore index (44% Manganese, CIF Tianjin)	415	324	262	291	243	163	246
Iron ore (China import, spot, CFR Tianjin port)	184	210	161	169	121	70	73
Aluminium (Primary, high grade, London Metal Exchange, cash)	140	155	130	119	120	107	103
Copper (Grade A, London Metal Exchange, cash)	406	458	418	391	347	300	301
Nickel (London Metal Exchange, cash)	252	265	203	174	195	137	111
Lead (London Metal Exchange, cash settlement)	462	498	433	456	424	389	464
Zinc (Special high grade, London Metal Exchange, cash settlement)	192	194	173	169	192	171	185
Tin (London Metal Exchange, cash)	375	480	388	411	403	296	324
Memo item							
Crude petroleum (Average of UK Brent, Dubai and Texas)	280	368	372	369	341	180	152

Note: Price indices based on United States dollars.

Population

KEY FIGURES 2016

World population
7.5 billion

Annual
population growth
+1.1%

Share of urban
population in
developing economies
49%

Child dependency
ratio in LDCs
71%

4.1 Total and urban population

Map 4.1 | **World population, 2016**

Population
(Millions)
----- 100
----- 10

Share of urban population
(Percentage)

- 90 to 100
- 70 to less than 90
- 50 to less than 70
- 30 to less than 50
- 0 to less than 30

Concepts and definitions

The population estimates and projections reported in this chapter represent the "de facto" population as of the 1st of July of a given year (United Nations, 2017b).

The figures for the years 2015–2050 are based on the medium variant projection. This assumes that the average fertility rate of the world will decline from 2.5 births per woman in 2010–2015 to 2.2 in 2045–2050. Future population growth is highly dependent on the path that future fertility will take. Relatively small changes in the frequency of childbearing, when projected over several decades, can generate large differences in total population (ibid.).

Urban population is defined as the "de facto" population living in areas classified as urban according to the criteria used by each country or territory (United Nations, 2017c).

Population growth rate decreasing over time

The world population growth rate has been declining since the end of the 1960s. In 1969, the world population increased by 2.1 per cent compared to the year before. Until 1979, the annual growth rate then fell to 1.8 per cent and remained at that level for the next nine years. After a further strong fall during the early 1990s, the rate reached 1.3 per cent at the turn of the millennium. Today it amounts to 1.1 per cent. It is projected to decrease further, down to 0.5 per cent by 2050.

Unequal distribution across countries

In 2016, the world population was 7.5 billion, with 58 per cent of people inhabiting only 10 economies. Three of the four most populated economies in the world were located in Asia: China, India and Indonesia. Jointly, they accounted for 40 per cent of the world total.

Figure 4.1.1 | **Annual growth rate of world population**
(Percentage)

Projection

Note: Annual exponential rate of growth of the population (see annex 6.3).

Developing economies drive population growth

Of the world population in 2016 (7.5 billion), 6.1 billion people, i.e. four fifths, lived in developing economies. In the middle of the last century, developing economies had accounted for only two thirds of the world population. Over the last six decades, this share increased as a consequence of relatively high population growth. The population of Africa has been expanding particularly strongly (in 2016, by 2.5 per cent), and it is forecast to do so also for the next three decades. By 2050, the global population is projected to reach almost 10 billion.

Figure 4.1.2 | **World population by group of economies** (Billions)

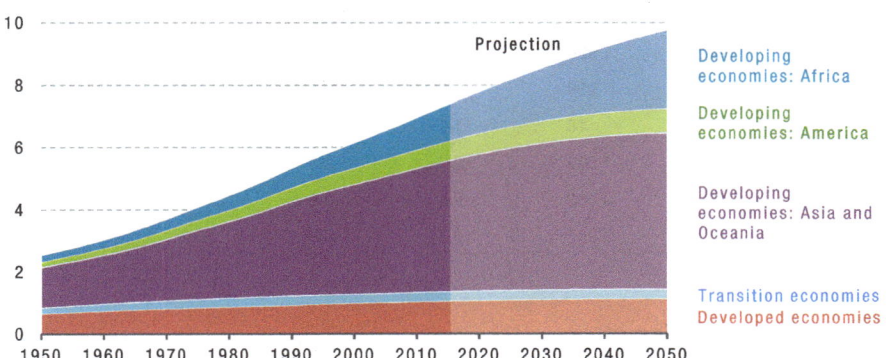

Urbanization continues

In 2016, the developing economies of America had the highest rate of urbanization (80%) of any developing region. In Africa, the urban population only accounted for 41 per cent of the population.

In the coming decades, urbanization is expected to increase considerably. Today, 54 per cent of the world population lives in urban areas. By 2050, this share is forecast to increase to 66 per cent. That equates to an additional 2.4 billion people living in urban centres – an increase of 193 000 persons per day for the next 33 years.

Figure 4.1.3 | **Urban population by group of economies, 2016** (Percentage of total population)

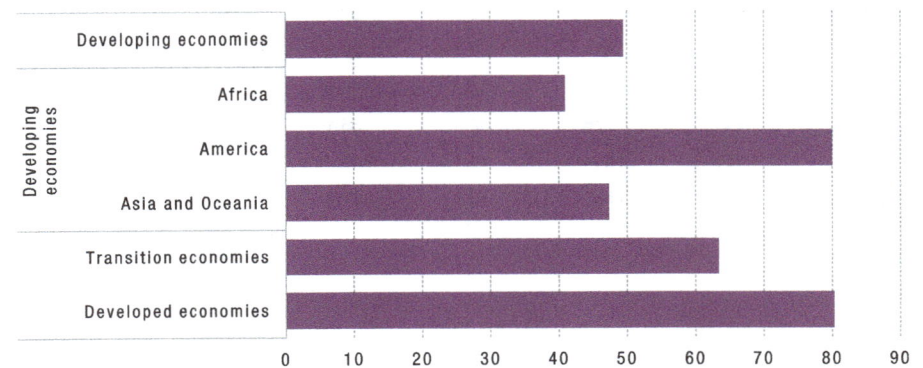

10 economies are home to **58% of the world's people**

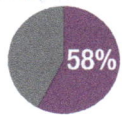

Four fifths of the global **population** live in **developing** economies

Africa's population increased by **2.5%** in 2016

In developing economies of **America 80% live** in **urban** centres

Table 4.1.1 | Total population by group of economies

Group of economies	Population (Millions)			Annual growth rate (Percentage)		
	2011	2016	2050	2011-2016	2016	2016-2050
World	**7 043**	**7 467**	**9 772**	**1.2**	**1.1**	**0.8**
Developing economies	5 709	6 109	8 342	1.4	1.3	0.9
Developing economies: Africa	1 076	1 224	2 526	2.6	2.5	2.1
Developing economies: America	600	634	775	1.1	1.1	0.6
Developing economies: Asia and Oceania	4 033	4 251	5 041	1.1	1.0	0.5
Transition economies	301	306	308	0.3	0.3	0.0
Developed economies	1 033	1 052	1 122	0.4	0.4	0.2
Selected groups						
Developing economies excluding China	4 341	4 705	6 978	1.6	1.6	1.2
Developing economies excluding LDCs	4 838	5 128	6 422	1.2	1.1	0.7
LDCs	870	981	1 920	2.4	2.4	2.0
LLDCs	425	492	939	2.9	2.4	1.9
SIDS (UNCTAD)	12	13	16	1.0	1.0	0.7
HIPCs (IMF)	596	686	1 502	2.8	2.8	2.3
BRICS	3 009	3 135	3 462	0.8	0.8	0.3
G20	4 337	4 519	5 057	0.8	0.8	0.3

Table 4.1.2 | Urban population by group of economies

Group of economies	Urban population (Millions)			Share in total population (Percentage)		
	2011	2016	2050	2011	2016	2050
World	**3 665**	**4 060**	**6 465**	**52.0**	**54.4**	**66.2**
Developing economies	2 657	3 022	5 275	46.5	49.5	63.2
Developing economies: Africa	417	501	1 418	38.7	40.9	56.1
Developing economies: America	472	507	669	78.6	80.0	86.4
Developing economies: Asia and Oceania	1 769	2 013	3 187	43.9	47.4	63.2
Transition economies	190	194	219	63.2	63.4	71.1
Developed economies	817	844	972	79.1	80.3	86.6
Selected groups						
Developing economies excluding China	1 966	2 225	4 240	45.3	47.3	60.8
Developing economies excluding LDCs	2 400	2 707	4 316	49.6	52.8	67.2
LDCs	257	315	959	29.5	32.1	50.0
LLDCs	120	144	411	28.1	29.3	43.7
SIDS (UNCTAD)	5	5	8	39.9	40.9	50.4
HIPCs (IMF)	195	241	776	32.8	35.1	51.6
BRICS	1 388	1 557	2 244	46.1	49.7	64.8
G20	2 386	2 618	3 589	55.0	57.9	71.0

Table 4.1.3 | Most populated economies by group

Developing economies: Africa

Economy	Total			Urban		
	Population (Millions)	Annual growth rate (Percentage)		Share in total population (Percentage)	Annual growth rate (Percentage)	
	2016	2011-2016	2016-2050	2016	2011-2016	2016-2050
Nigeria	186	2.7	2.3	48.6	4.5	3.3
Ethiopia	102	2.6	1.8	19.9	4.9	3.7
Egypt	96	2.2	1.4	43.2	2.3	2.2
Dem. Rep. of the Congo	79	3.3	2.7	43.0	4.5	3.7
South Africa	56	1.4	0.8	65.3	2.2	1.3
Developing Africa	**1 224**	**2.6**	**2.1**	**40.9**	**3.7**	**3.1**

Developing economies: America

Economy	Total			Urban		
	Population (Millions)	Annual growth rate (Percentage)		Share in total population (Percentage)	Annual growth rate (Percentage)	
	2016	2011-2016	2016-2050	2016	2011-2016	2016-2050
Brazil	208	0.9	0.3	85.9	1.2	0.5
Mexico	128	1.4	0.7	79.5	1.7	1.0
Colombia	49	0.9	0.3	76.7	1.3	0.6
Argentina	44	1.0	0.7	91.9	1.2	0.8
Peru	32	1.3	0.8	78.9	1.7	1.1
Developing America	**634**	**1.1**	**0.6**	**80.0**	**1.5**	**0.8**

Developing economies: Asia and Oceania

Economy	Total			Urban		
	Population (Millions)	Annual growth rate (Percentage)		Share in total population (Percentage)	Annual growth rate (Percentage)	
	2016	2011-2016	2016-2050	2016	2011-2016	2016-2050
China	1 404	0.5	-0.1	56.8	2.8	0.8
India	1 324	1.2	0.7	33.1	2.4	1.9
Indonesia	261	1.2	0.6	54.5	2.6	1.4
Pakistan	193	2.1	1.4	39.2	3.2	2.5
Bangladesh	163	1.1	0.6	35.0	3.4	2.0
Developing Asia and Oceania	**4 251**	**1.1**	**0.5**	**47.4**	**2.6**	**1.4**

4.2 Age structure

Map 4.2 | **Dependency ratio, 2016**
(Percentage)

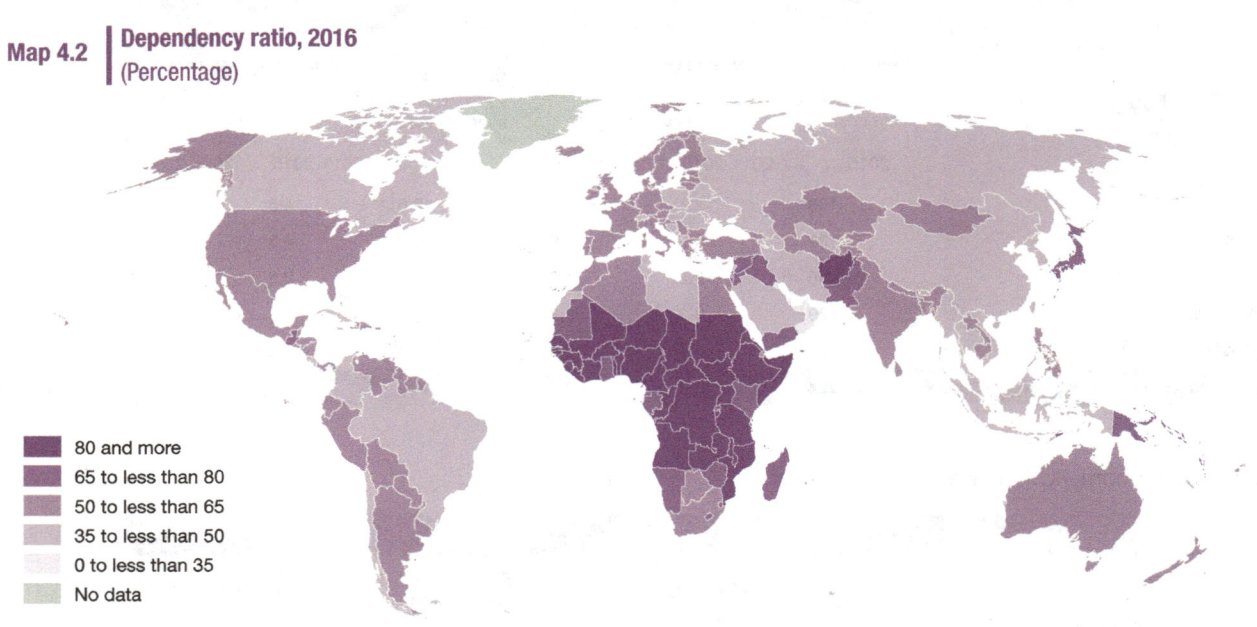

- 80 and more
- 65 to less than 80
- 50 to less than 65
- 35 to less than 50
- 0 to less than 35
- No data

Concepts and definitions

In this section, the term "persons of working age" refers to persons aged from 15 to 64 years. The term "children" refers to persons under the age of 15. The term "older persons" refers to persons aged 65 years or more.

The dependency ratio is defined as the number of children and older persons per hundred persons of working age. It can be expressed as the sum of the child dependency ratio and the old-age dependency ratio.

The child dependency ratio is defined as the number of children per hundred persons of working age.

The old-age dependency ratio is defined as the number of older persons per hundred persons of working age.

Aging of the world population

In 2016, 66 per cent of the global population were of working age (15 to 64 years old), 26 per cent were children and 8 per cent were 65 years or older. Since the 1960s, the share of children has steadily decreased while the share of older persons has increased. This trend is forecast to continue. According to projections, by the year 2050, 21 per cent of the population will be under the age of 16, and 16 per cent will be older than 64 years.

Dependency ratios throughout the world

In 2016, the highest ratio of non-working age to working age population was found in sub-Saharan Africa and Afghanistan. This was reflected in dependency ratios higher than 80 per cent. In most developed economies the ratio ranged between 50 and 65 per cent.

Figure 4.2.1 | **World population by age group**
(Billions)

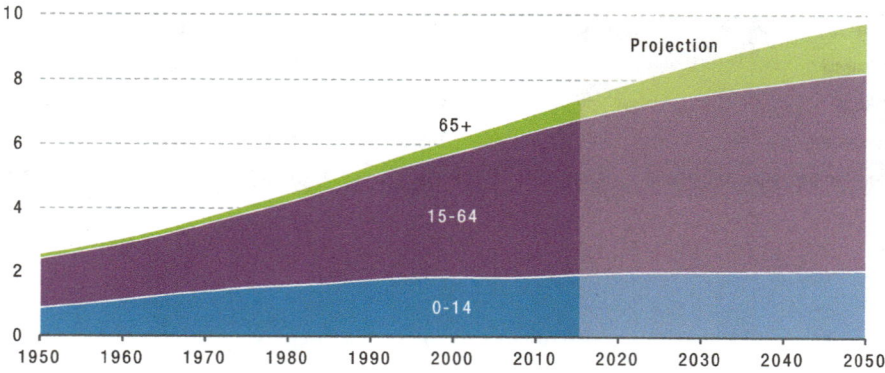

Age and gender structure in detail

The population pyramid of developing economies has a triangular shape, as the highest population shares are found in the younger age classes and population shares diminish for older age classes. The population pyramid of developed economies is bell shaped due to substantially smaller relative proportions of young people. In 2016, the largest age class in developed economies was 50 to 54 years. Half of the population was more than 40 years old, whereas in developing economies this was the case for only one third.

Figure 4.2.2 | Population pyramids, 2016

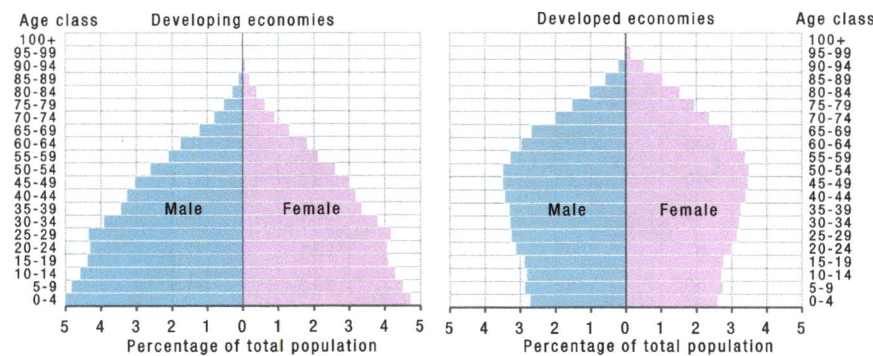

Differences in the structure of dependency

While the total dependency ratio of developing and developed economies was similarly high in 2016 – around 53 per cent – the underlying structure was entirely different. Developing economies showed a comparatively high share of child dependency, as reflected by the triangular shape of the age pyramid, whereas in developed economies dependency concerns mainly older persons. As a result of population ageing, in 2050, developed economies are projected to have a higher overall dependency ratio than Africa.

Figure 4.2.3 | Dependency ratio by age structure (Percentage)

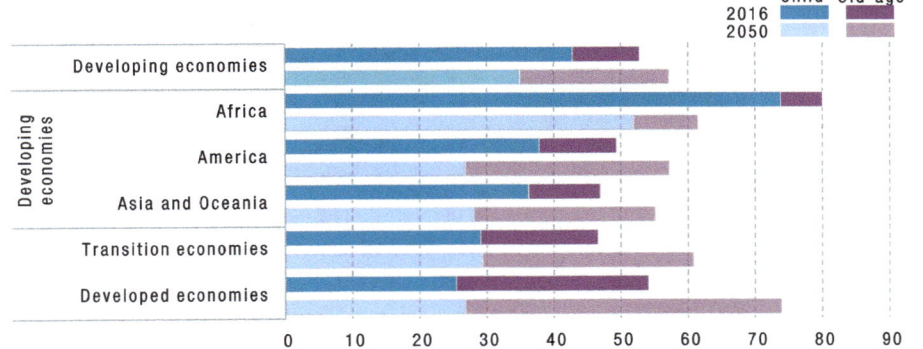

Note: The total dependency ratio is the sum of the child and old-age dependency ratios.

66% of the global **population** was of **working age** in 2016

In **Africa,** the **dependency ratio** is **80%**

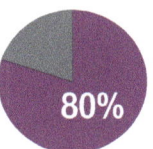
80%

Greater proportion of **young people** living **in developing** economies than developed

In **developed** economies **old-age** dependency is **high** - and **increasing**

Table 4.2.1 | Age structure by group of economies

Group of economies	Year	Population (Millions)			Dependency ratio (Percentage)		
		0-14	15-64	65+	Child (0-14)	Old-age (65+)	Total
World	2011	**1 876**	**4 620**	**545**	**40.6**	**11.8**	**52.4**
	2016	**1 944**	**4 888**	**633**	**39.8**	**13.0**	**52.7**
	2050	**2 083**	**6 142**	**1 546**	**33.9**	**25.2**	**59.1**
Developing economies	2011	1 647	3 724	337	44.2	9.1	53.3
	2016	1 710	3 997	401	42.8	10.0	52.8
	2050	1 854	5 306	1 182	34.9	22.3	57.2
Developing economies: Africa	2011	445	594	37	75.0	6.2	81.2
	2016	502	680	43	73.8	6.3	80.0
	2050	811	1 564	150	51.9	9.6	61.5
Developing economies: America	2011	163	395	41	41.3	10.4	51.7
	2016	160	424	49	37.8	11.6	49.4
	2050	132	493	150	26.8	30.4	57.2
Developing economies: Asia and Oceania	2011	1 038	2 735	260	37.9	9.5	47.4
	2016	1 048	2 893	309	36.2	10.7	46.9
	2050	910	3 249	881	28.0	27.1	55.1
Transition economies	2011	55	211	35	26.2	16.5	42.6
	2016	61	209	36	29.1	17.5	46.5
	2050	56	192	60	29.3	31.5	60.8
Developed economies	2011	175	685	173	25.5	25.3	50.7
	2016	173	682	196	25.4	28.7	54.1
	2050	173	645	304	26.8	47.1	73.9
Selected groups							
Developing economies excluding China	2011	1 405	2 716	220	51.7	8.1	59.8
	2016	1 461	2 984	259	49.0	8.7	57.7
	2050	1 663	4 491	823	37.0	18.3	55.3
Developing economies excluding LDCs	2011	1 288	3 242	307	39.7	9.5	49.2
	2016	1 319	3 443	366	38.3	10.6	48.9
	2050	1 267	4 099	1 056	30.9	25.8	56.7
LDCs	2011	359	482	30	74.5	6.3	80.7
	2016	391	555	35	70.5	6.3	76.8
	2050	587	1 207	126	48.6	10.4	59.0
LLDCs	2011	173	237	16	72.9	6.5	79.5
	2016	195	279	18	69.7	6.5	76.2
	2050	280	597	62	46.9	10.3	57.2
SIDS (UNCTAD)	2011	3	7	1	46.4	10.2	56.6
	2016	3	8	1	43.4	11.2	54.6
	2050	3	10	2	35.2	22.8	58.0
HIPCs (IMF)	2011	265	313	18	84.7	5.8	90.6
	2016	297	367	21	80.9	5.8	86.7
	2050	495	931	76	53.1	8.2	61.4
BRICS	2011	708	2 083	218	34.0	10.4	44.4
	2016	709	2 167	259	32.7	11.9	44.7
	2050	576	2 213	672	26.0	30.4	56.4
G20	2011	993	2 961	383	33.5	12.9	46.5
	2016	994	3 077	448	32.3	14.6	46.9
	2050	844	3 184	1 030	26.5	32.3	58.8

Table 4.2.2 | **Age structure by gender and group of economies, 2016**

Group of economies	Gender	Population (Millions)	Age class (Percentage)					
			0-14	15-24	25-39	40-64	65-74	75+
World	**Female**	**3 700**	**25.4**	**15.6**	**22.4**	**27.2**	**5.5**	**3.9**
	Male	**3 766**	**26.7**	**16.3**	**22.8**	**26.7**	**4.8**	**2.7**
Developing economies	Female	3 004	27.5	16.6	23.0	25.8	4.5	2.6
	Male	3 104	28.5	17.1	23.1	25.2	4.0	2.0
Developing economies: Africa	Female	613	40.4	19.1	20.5	16.2	2.6	1.2
	Male	611	41.6	19.4	20.4	15.5	2.2	0.9
Developing economies: America	Female	320	24.5	16.9	23.4	26.6	5.0	3.6
	Male	313	26.1	17.8	23.9	25.3	4.4	2.5
Developing economies: Asia and Oceania	Female	2 071	24.1	15.8	23.6	28.6	5.0	2.9
	Male	2 179	25.2	16.4	23.7	28.0	4.5	2.2
Transition economies	Female	161	18.3	11.4	22.9	32.6	7.4	7.4
	Male	145	21.5	13.3	25.5	31.0	5.2	3.5
Developed economies	Female	535	15.8	11.3	19.0	33.3	10.4	10.2
	Male	517	17.2	12.2	20.1	33.9	9.6	7.0
Selected groups								
Developing economies excluding China	Female	2 324	30.6	17.9	22.8	22.6	3.8	2.2
	Male	2 381	31.6	18.5	23.0	22.0	3.3	1.6
Developing economies excluding LDCs	Female	2 512	25.2	16.0	23.4	27.7	4.9	2.9
	Male	2 615	26.3	16.6	23.6	27.0	4.4	2.2
LDCs	Female	492	39.3	19.7	20.7	16.5	2.6	1.3
	Male	489	40.5	20.1	20.3	15.8	2.3	1.0
LLDCs	Female	247	38.7	19.6	20.8	16.7	2.7	1.5
	Male	245	40.4	20.1	20.6	15.7	2.2	1.1
SIDS (UNCTAD)	Female	6	27.6	17.6	22.1	24.8	4.7	3.3
	Male	6	28.6	18.2	22.5	24.2	4.2	2.3
HIPCs (IMF)	Female	344	42.8	19.9	19.5	14.5	2.3	1.1
	Male	342	43.9	20.2	19.3	13.7	2.0	0.8
BRICS	Female	1 529	21.9	14.8	23.6	30.7	5.6	3.4
	Male	1 606	23.3	15.6	23.9	29.7	5.0	2.5
G20	Female	2 225	21.3	14.4	22.7	30.6	6.4	4.6
	Male	2 294	22.7	15.2	23.2	30.0	5.7	3.2

Maritime Transport

KEY FIGURES **2016**

Internationally
shipped goods

10.3 billion

metric tons

World commercial
fleet (as of 31 December)

1.9 billion

dead-weight tons

Growth in
commercial fleet
shipping capacity

+3.1%

Global container
port traffic

701 million

twenty-foot equivalent units

5.1 World seaborne trade

Map 5.1 | **Tonnage loaded and unloaded, 2016**
| (Billions of metric tons)

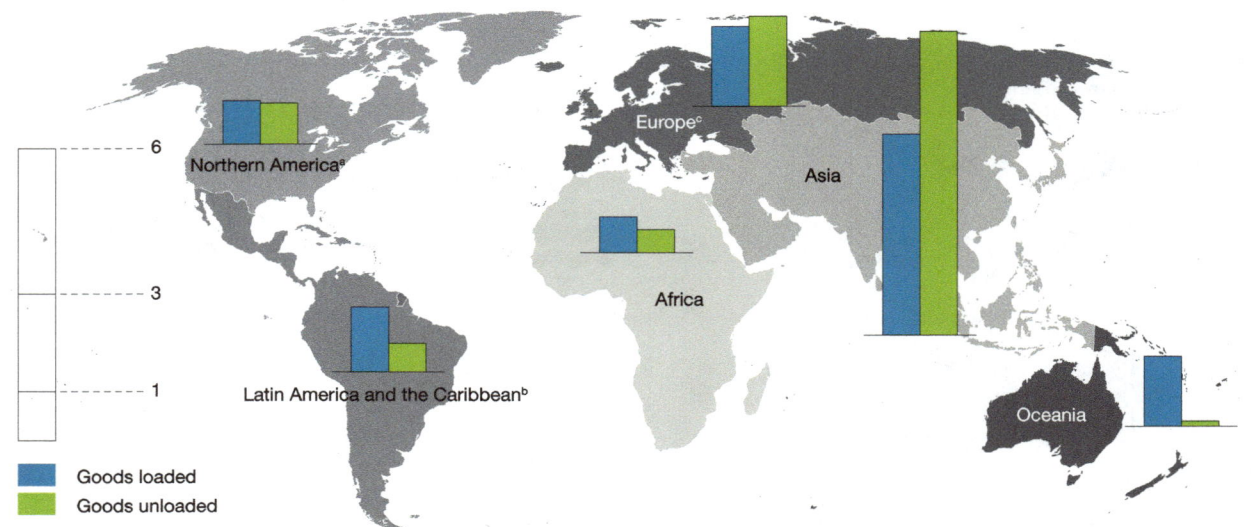

a Equal to the group 'Developed economies: America' on UNCTADstat.
b Equal to the group 'Developing economies: America' on UNCTADstat.
c Incl. the Russian Federation and the French overseas departments.

Concepts and definitions

The figures on seaborne trade in this section measure the volumes, in metric tons, of goods loaded and unloaded in the world's seaports for international shipment. Cabotage and transshipments are not included.

The data have been compiled from various sources including country reports as well as port industry and other specialist websites.

Surpluses or deficits in volume terms are not necessarily related to commercial balances of payments, as different types of cargo may have different monetary value per metric ton.

Goods loaded for international shipment are assumed to be exports, while goods unloaded from ships are assumed to be imports.

The seaborne trade balance measures the difference between the volumes of loaded and unloaded goods.

Trends and geography of world seaborne trade

World seaborne trade reached 10.3 billion tons in 2016 after a steady increase over the last seven years. Since 2009, the volume of goods loaded and unloaded in ports worldwide has grown by 2.4 billion tons. In particular the trade of dry cargo and petroleum products and gas by sea has increased.

Asia is by far the largest trading region. In 2016, 4.1 billion tons of goods were loaded and 6.3 billion tons of goods were unloaded in Asian seaports. The other continents registered less than half of these amounts.

Contrary to Asia, in Oceania, in Latin America and the Caribbean, and in Africa, more goods were loaded than unloaded. The volumes of goods delivered to ports in Oceania were, at less than 200 million metric tons, particularly small.

Figure 5.1.1 | **Goods loaded worldwide**
| (Billions of metric tons)

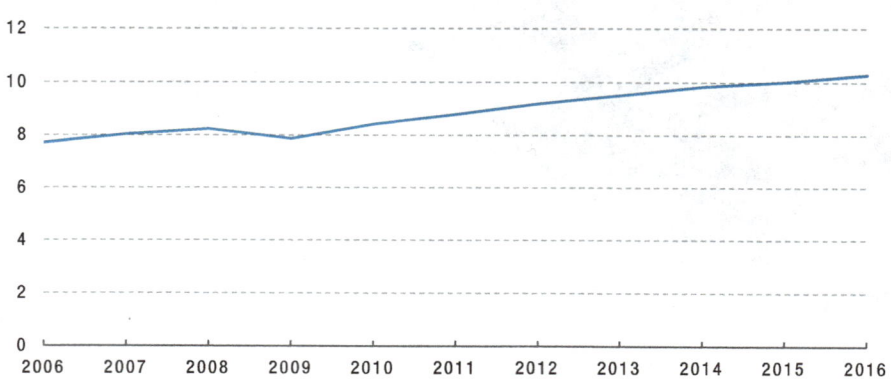

Contribution of developing economies

Developing economies, as a group, are a strong contributor to world seaborne trade. In 2016, they accounted for 59 per cent of total goods loaded and for 64 per cent of total goods unloaded. Their share in goods loaded has decreased slightly over the last ten years, whereas their share in goods unloaded has grown considerably: in 2006, less than half of the goods shipped worldwide were destined for seaports in developing economies; by 2016, this had increased to almost two thirds.

Figure 5.1.2 | **Seaborne trade of developing economies**
(Percentage of corresponding world tonnage)

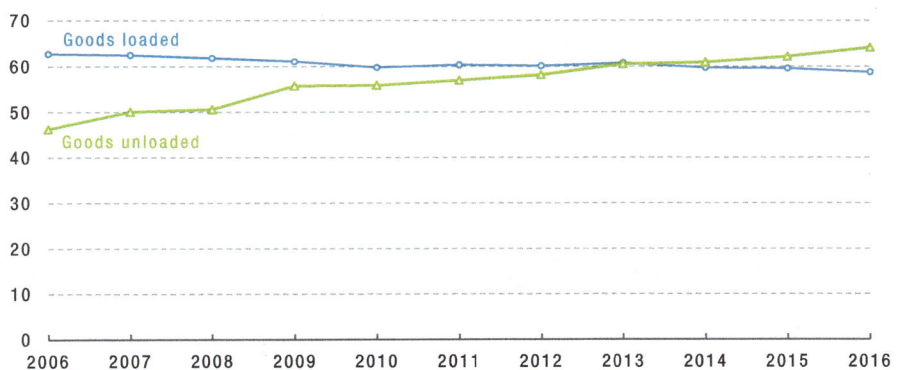

World **seaborne trade** amounts to **10.3 billion tons** in 2016

61% of goods delivered by sea are **unloaded** in **Asian seaports**

Developments in seaborne trade balances

In 2014, developing economies turned from net exporters into net importers of seaborne trade volumes. In 2016, they recorded 541 million tons more of goods unloaded than of goods loaded.

Transition economies have increased their seaborne trade surplus over the last five years, due to a strong growth of dry cargo loaded (from 331 million to 422 million tons) and a considerable drop of dry cargo unloaded (from 148 million to 57 million tons). The seaborne trade of developed economies is currently in balance.[1]

[1] For further analyses on that topic, see UNCTAD (2017c).

Figure 5.1.3 | **Seaborne trade balance**
(Millions of metric tons)

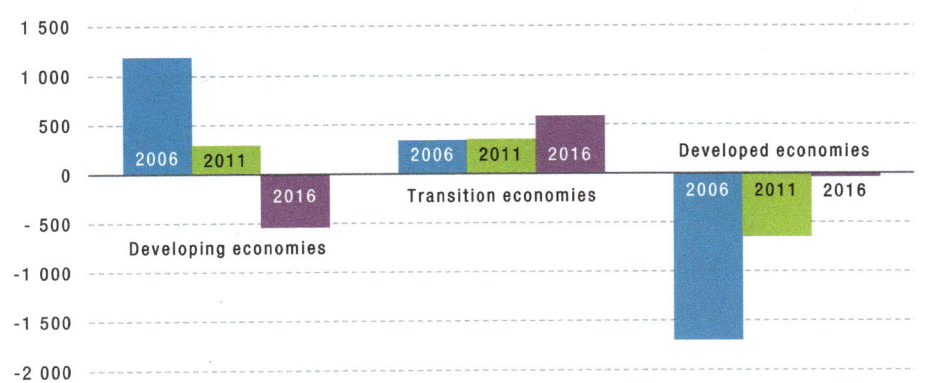

Developing economies: **unloading exceeds** loading by **541 million tons**

Seaborne trade for **developed** economies currently **in balance**

Table 5.1.1 | Total seaborne trade by group of economies

Group of economies	Loaded			Unloaded			Balance	
	Volume		Annual growth rate	Volume		Annual growth rate	Volume	
	(Millions of metric tons)		(Percentage)	(Millions of metric tons)		(Percentage)	(Millions of metric tons)	
	2011	2016	2016	2011	2016	2016	2011	2016
World[a]	**8 784**	**10 287**	**2.6**	**8 798**	**10 282**	**2.6**	**-13**	**5**
Developing economies	5 297	6 046	1.2	5 009	6 587	5.8	288	-541
Developing economies: Africa	724	745	-1.3	378	506	4.2	346	239
Developing economies: America	1 239	1 369	3.1	508	594	0.8	731	775
Developing economies: Asia and Oceania	3 334	3 931	1.0	4 122	5 487	6.6	-788	-1 555
Transition economies	505	646	2.2	157	62	4.9	348	585
Developed economies	2 982	3 595	5.2	3 632	3 633	-2.7	-650	-38

[a] Annual totals of goods loaded and unloaded are not necessarily the same, given that goods loaded in one calendar year may reach their port of destination in the next calendar year.

Table 5.1.2 | Seaborne trade by cargo type and group of economies

Crude oil

Group of economies	Loaded			Unloaded			Balance	
	Volume		Annual growth rate	Volume		Annual growth rate	Volume	
	(Millions of metric tons)		(Percentage)	(Millions of metric tons)		(Percentage)	(Millions of metric tons)	
	2011	2016	2016	2011	2016	2016	2011	2016
World[a]	**1 759**	**1 838**	**4.3**	**1 897**	**1 990**	**4.2**	**-137**	**-152**
Developing economies	1 509	1 518	3.5	807	999	9.1	703	519
Developing economies: Africa	338	290	-1.2	38	40	1.9	300	250
Developing economies: America	254	271	21.1	71	58	-11.5	183	213
Developing economies: Asia and Oceania	918	957	0.8	698	901	11.1	220	56
Transition economies	133	176	7.3	4	0	9.9	128	176
Developed economies	117	144	10.7	1 086	991	-0.3	-968	-847

[a] Annual totals of goods loaded and unloaded are not necessarily the same, given that goods loaded in one calendar year may reach their port of destination in the next calendar year.

Petroleum product and gas

Group of economies	Loaded			Unloaded			Balance	
	Volume		Annual growth rate	Volume		Annual growth rate	Volume	
	(Millions of metric tons)		(Percentage)	(Millions of metric tons)		(Percentage)	(Millions of metric tons)	
	2011	2016	2016	2011	2016	2016	2011	2016
World[a]	**1 034**	**1 218**	**4.0**	**1 038**	**1 233**	**3.9**	**-4**	**-15**
Developing economies	540	665	0.6	452	695	6.7	88	-31
Developing economies: Africa	69	50	-14.3	46	79	9.2	22	-29
Developing economies: America	83	70	-16.9	74	123	20.5	10	-53
Developing economies: Asia and Oceania	388	545	5.2	332	494	3.3	56	51
Transition economies	42	48	11.8	4	4	2.9	38	44
Developed economies	452	505	8.1	581	533	0.5	-129	-28

[a] Annual totals of goods loaded and unloaded are not necessarily the same, given that goods loaded in one calendar year may reach their port of destination in the next calendar year.

Dry cargo

Group of economies	Loaded			Unloaded			Balance	
	Volume		Annual growth rate	Volume		Annual growth rate	Volume	
	(Millions of metric tons)		(Percentage)	(Millions of metric tons)		(Percentage)	(Millions of metric tons)	
	2011	2016	2016	2011	2016	2016	2011	2016
World[a]	**5 991**	**7 231**	**2.0**	**5 863**	**7 058**	**2.0**	**127**	**173**
Developing economies	3 247	3 863	0.4	3 750	4 893	5.1	-503	-1 030
Developing economies: Africa	317	405	0.5	294	387	3.5	23	18
Developing economies: America	902	1 029	0.8	363	413	-2.0	539	616
Developing economies: Asia and Oceania	2 028	2 430	0.3	3 093	4 092	6.0	-1 065	-1 663
Transition economies	331	422	-0.7	148	57	5.1	182	365
Developed economies	2 413	2 946	4.5	1 965	2 109	-4.5	448	838

[a] Annual totals of goods loaded and unloaded are not necessarily the same, given that goods loaded in one calendar year may reach their port of destination in the next calendar year.

Table 5.1.3 | **Development of goods loaded worldwide by type of cargo**
(Millions of metric tons)

Year	Total goods	Crude oil	Petroleum products and gas	Dry cargo
1971	2 692	1 210	320	1 162
1976	3 366	1 555	289	1 522
1981	3 555	1 364	327	1 864
1986	3 385	1 126	424	1 835
1991	4 120	1 333	457	2 330
1996	4 758	1 590	537	2 631
2001	6 020	1 678	499	3 844
2006	7 700	1 783	915	5 002
2011	8 784	1 759	1 034	5 991
2016	10 287	1 838	1 218	7 231

5.2 Merchant fleet

Map 5.2 | **Building, ownership, registration and scrapping of ships, 2016**
(Percentage of world total)

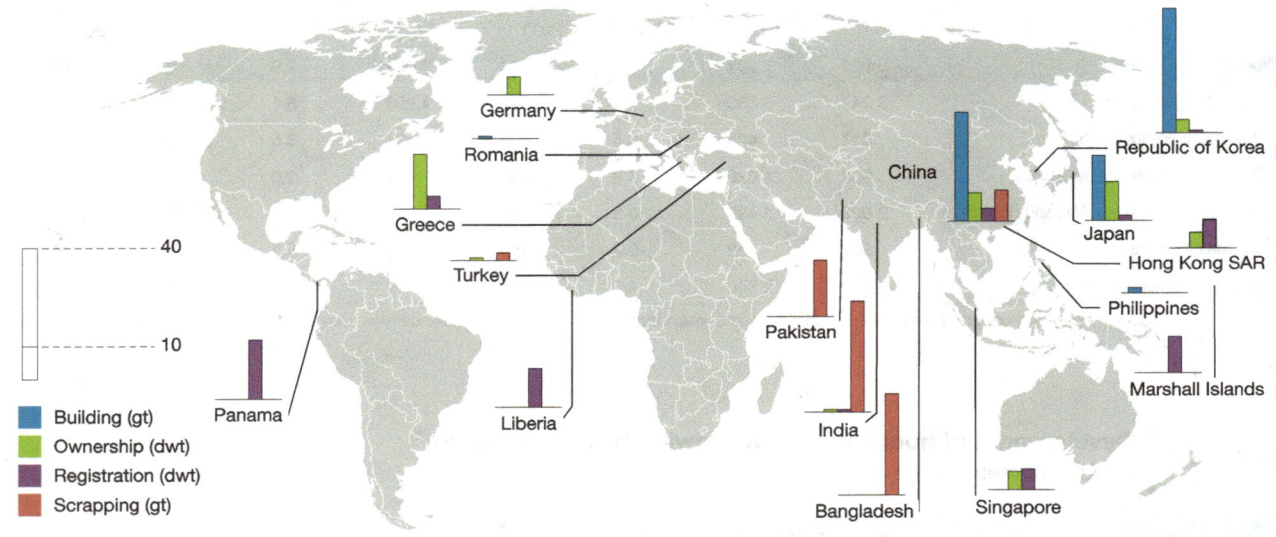

Note: Top five countries in each segment are shown. Building and scrapping are estimated deliveries and demolitions during 2016. Registration and ownership are end-of-year figures.

Concepts and definitions

Dead-weight tons (dwt) reflect the cargo carrying capacity of a ship, while gross tons (gt) reflect its size. The latter is relevant to measure shipbuilding and scrapping activity, while the former is used to capture the capacity to transport international trade volumes.

Statistics on fleet registration (the flag of a ship), shipbuilding and scrapping is for all commercial ships of 100 gt and more, while the market shares for ownership only cover larger ships of 1000 gt and above, as the true ownership is not always known for smaller vessels.

World fleet continuously growing

The world fleet has grown continuously since the beginning of the 1990s. This growth accelerated in 2005. As a result, in 2017, the world fleet reached 1.9 billion dwt, twice the size as it had 12 years ago. Today, bulk carriers account for 43 per cent of the fleet, followed by oil tankers (29 per cent) and container ships (13 per cent).

The top five ship owners at the end of 2016 were Greece, Japan, China, Germany and Singapore; together they had a market share of 50 per cent in dead-weight tons. The top five flag registries were Panama, Liberia, the Marshall Islands, Hong Kong SAR, and Singapore. Only three economies, the Republic of Korea, China, and Japan, constructed 92 per cent of world tonnage in 2016. Four economies, India, Bangladesh, Pakistan and China, together accounted for 95 per cent of ship scrapping in 2016.

Figure 5.2.1 | **World fleet by principal vessel type**
(Millions of dead-weight tons)

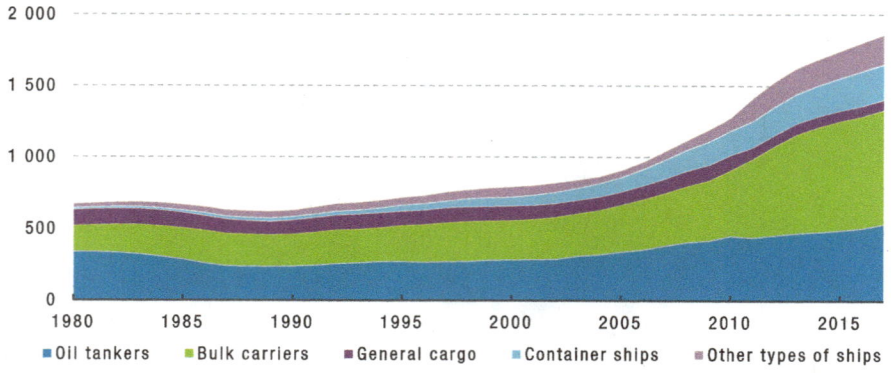

Sources: UNCTADstat (UNCTAD, 2017a); Clarksons Research.

Fleet ownership by region

Asian economies have the highest market share in shipowning (49 per cent), followed by Europe (41 per cent) and Northern America (7 per cent). Latin America and the Caribbean (1 per cent), Africa (1 per cent) and Oceania (close to 0 per cent) continue to have only small market shares. Looking at ship registration, however, developing economies in Africa and America play a more important role, accounting for 7 and 17 per cent of registrations (in dead-weight tons), respectively.

Figure 5.2.2 | **Fleet market share by region of beneficial ownership, 2017***
| (Dead-weight tons)

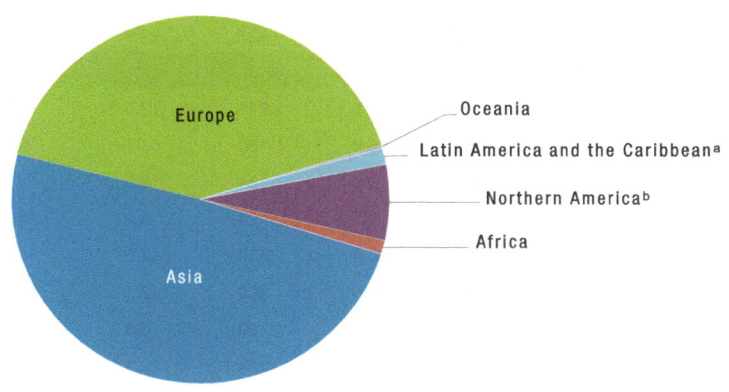

* As of 1 January.
[a] Equal to the group 'Developing economies: America' on UNCTADstat.
[b] Equal to the group 'Developed economies: America' on UNCTADstat.
Source: UNCTADstat (UNCTAD, 2017a); Clarksons Research.

Major flags of registration

Important countries of ship registration are often small developing economies in Africa, America and the Pacific. Panama has maintained its position as the largest flag of registration for more than 20 years. At the beginning of 2017, its registered fleet reached 343 million dwt. Panama is followed by Liberia (219 million dwt), the Marshall Islands (217 million dwt), Hong Kong SAR (173 million dwt) and Singapore (124 million dwt). The Marshall Islands recorded the highest growth rate among the major registries over last 20 years.[1]

[1] For further analyses on that topic, see UNCTAD (2017c).

Figure 5.2.3 | **Vessels capacity in top 5 registries***
| (Millions of dead-weight tons)

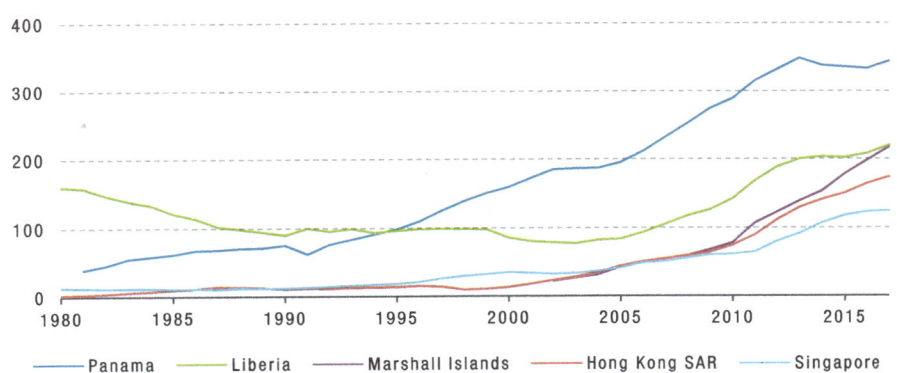

* Ranked by the values as of 1 January 2017.
Sources: UNCTADstat (UNCTAD, 2017a); Clarksons Research.

World fleet size reached **1.9 billion dwt** in 2017

92% of global **ship building** takes place in **three Asian** economies

One half of the world fleet is **owned** by entities from **Asia**

Panama, Liberia and the **Marshal Islands** take the **lead** in ship **registrations**

Table 5.2.1 | **Merchant fleet registration by group of economies**

Group of economies	2012				2017			
	Tonnage		Vessels		Tonnage		Vessels	
	(Millions of dwt)	Share in world (Percentage)	(Thousands)	Share in world (Percentage)	(Millions of dwt)	Share in world (Percentage)	(Thousands)	Share in world (Percentage)
World	**1 532**	**100.0**	**85**	**100.0**	**1 862**	**100.0**	**93**	**100.0**
Developing economies	1 140	74.4	54	64.1	1 420	76.2	62	66.4
Developing economies: Africa	201	13.1	6	6.6	236	12.7	7	7.0
Developing economies: America	447	29.2	17	19.6	462	24.8	16	17.4
Developing economies: Asia and Oceania	492	32.1	32	37.9	721	38.8	39	41.9
Transition economies	9	0.6	4	4.3	11	0.6	4	4.1
Developed economies	378	24.6	26	30.3	427	22.9	26	27.8
Selected groups								
Developing economies excluding China	1 078	70.4	51	59.9	1 341	72.0	58	61.8
Developing economies excluding LDCs	939	61.3	48	56.9	1 186	63.7	55	59.3
LDCs	201	13.1	6	7.2	234	12.5	7	7.0
LLDCs	3	0.2	1	1.1	4	0.2	1	1.2
SIDS (UNCTAD)	226	14.8	7	8.9	320	17.2	8	9.1
HIPCs (IMF)	193	12.6	5	5.8	226	12.1	5	5.9
BRICS	89	5.8	8	9.3	109	5.8	9	10.1
G20	259	16.9	33	38.6	284	15.3	37	39.4

Sources: UNCTADstat (UNCTAD, 2017a); Clarksons Research.
Note: Commercial ships of 100 gt and above; beginning-of-year figures.

Table 5.2.2 | **Fleet ownership and registration, main economies, 1 January 2017**

Vessels
(Number of vessels)

Economy of ownership (Ranked by number of ships owned)	Flag of registration (Ranked by number of ships registered)							
	Panama	China	Liberia	Marshall Islands	Singapore	China, Hong Kong SAR	Malta	World
China	559	3 256	41	28	51	770	20	**5 206**
Greece	420	0	842	820	37	21	622	**4 199**
Japan	2 225	0	156	146	123	68	8	**3 901**
Germany	29	0	904	176	58	20	177	**3 090**
Singapore	222	1	136	123	1 486	108	12	**2 599**
United States	99	0	93	386	9	68	29	**2 106**
Norway	55	0	41	138	88	33	88	**1 842**
Indonesia	21	1	6	1	12	3	0	**1 840**
Russian Federation	28	0	122	4	2	1	32	**1 707**
Korea, Republic of	534	0	1	222	3	22	5	**1 656**
World	**6 543**	**3 323**	**3 251**	**3 125**	**2 641**	**2 320**	**2 052**	**50 155**

Sources: UNCTADstat (UNCTAD, 2017a); Clarksons Research.
Note: Commercial ships of 1000 gt and above.

Tonnage
(Dead-weight tons)

Economy of ownership (Ranked by tonnage owned)	Flag of registration (Ranked by tonnage registered)							
	Panama	Liberia	Marshall Islands	China, Hong Kong SAR	Singapore	Malta	Bahamas	World
Greece	22 626	61 274	59 593	1 304	3 067	51 809	17 688	**308 837**
Japan	143 081	13 168	9 359	3 076	6 509	383	8 188	**223 856**
China	21 623	2 799	1 058	52 748	4 485	1 800	98	**165 430**
Germany	1 766	48 393	9 266	1 342	2 393	7 299	528	**112 028**
Singapore	7 530	8 773	8 204	5 598	63 676	119	552	**104 414**
China, Hong Kong SAR	8 717	4 005	2 069	71 173	3 763	398	61	**93 630**
Korea, Republic of	41 290	106	20 895	845	54	128	208	**80 977**
United States	3 962	7 471	29 872	4 299	393	979	4 253	**67 103**
Norway	2 538	1 787	6 866	5 785	1 981	1 080	4 987	**51 824**
United Kingdom	4 494	12 623	5 534	637	1 752	4 676	4 926	**51 648**
World	**342 792**	**219 379**	**216 594**	**173 257**	**123 986**	**99 184**	**79 825**	**1 847 631**

Sources: UNCTADstat (UNCTAD, 2017a); Clarksons Research.
Note: Commercial ships of 1000 gt and above.

5.3 Maritime transport indicators

Map 5.3 | Liner shipping connectivity, 2016

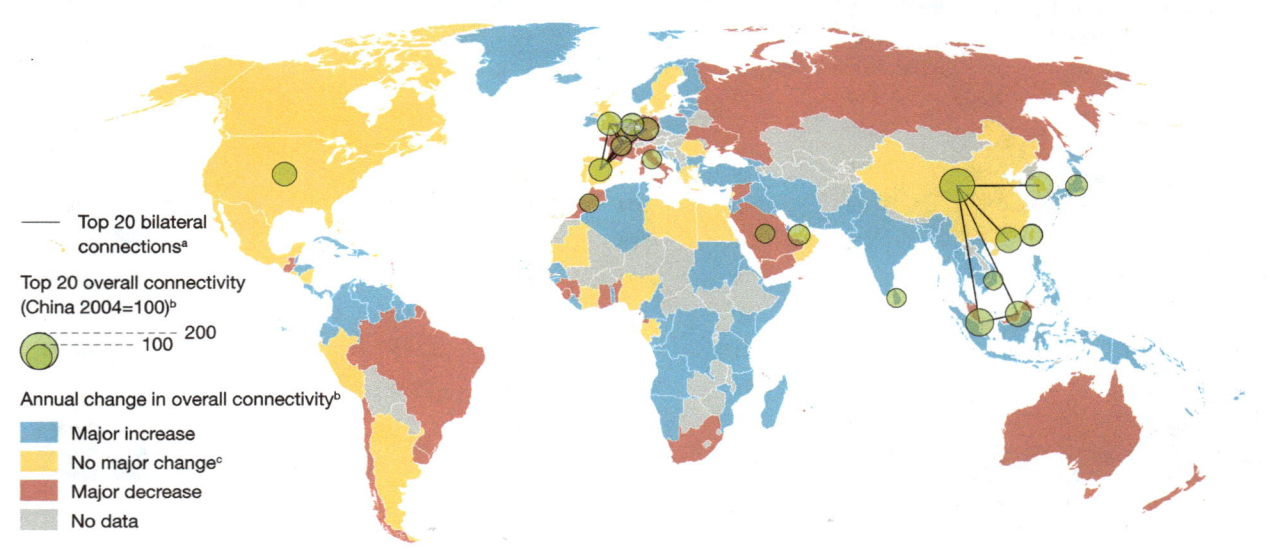

 Top 20 bilateral connections[a]

Top 20 overall connectivity (China 2004=100)[b]

100 — 200

Annual change in overall connectivity[b]

- **Major increase** (blue)
- **No major change[c]** (yellow)
- **Major decrease** (red)
- **No data** (grey)

[a] As indicated by the LSBCI.
[b] As indicated by the LSCI.
[c] Change of less than 5% compared to the value in the previous year.

Concepts and definitions

The UNCTAD liner shipping connectivity index (LSCI) is an indicator of a country's position within the global liner shipping networks. It is calculated from data on the world's container ship deployment: the number of ships, their container carrying capacity, the number of services and companies, and the size of the largest ship.

The liner shipping bilateral connectivity index (LSBCI) is calculated from five components that also take into account the number of transshipments required to trade as well as the number of options available to trade with only one transshipment.

Port container traffic is measured in twenty-foot equivalent units (TEU). A TEU represents the volume of a standard 20 feet long intermodal container used for loading, unloading, repositioning and transshipment.

Liner shipping connectivity throughout the world

The economy best connected to the global liner shipping network in 2016 was China, followed by Singapore, the Republic of Korea, Malaysia, Hong Kong SAR, the United Kingdom and the United States of America. Sub-regional leaders include Panama in Latin America, Morocco in Africa, and Sri Lanka in South Asia. The Russian Federation is the best connected transition economy. Within Europe and Eastern and South-Eastern Asia, economies are particularly closely connected with each other by shipping lines.

Trends in port container traffic

In 2016, 701 million TEUs of containers were handled on ports worldwide. World container port throughput has continuously increased over the last six years, since 2014, however, at a slower pace than before.

Figure 5.3.1 | **World container port throughput** (Millions of TEUs)

800

700

600

500

400

2010 2011 2012 2013 2014 2015 2016

Trends among the most connected economies

In recent years, liner shipping connectivity of the top-5 economies remained steady, following several years of strong growth. The LSCI of the world leader, China, which from 2004 to 2014 had increased on average by 6.5 points each year, went up by only 2.0 points between 2014 and 2015 and by 3.7 points between 2015 and 2016. Hong Kong SAR (-16.3) and Malaysia (-8.1) recorded a drop in LSCI levels between 2015 and 2016, while the LSCI of the Republic of Korea remained almost unchanged (-0.6).

China, Singapore and the **Republic of Korea** are **best integrated** into the global liner **shipping networks**

Figure 5.3.2 | **Liner shipping connectivity index, top five economies** (China 2004=100)

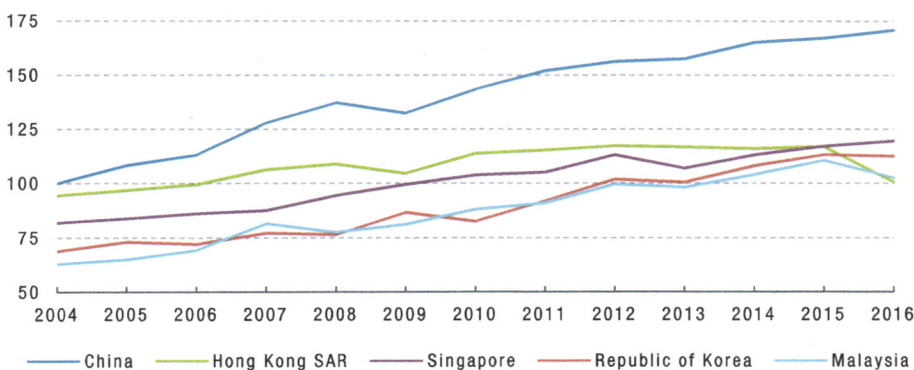

World **container port throughput** reached **701 million TEUs** in 2016

Port container throughput by group of economies

Asia's role as an important port loading and unloading area (see section 5.1) and its high liner shipping connectivity (see above) is also reflected in the region's high contribution to containerized port throughput. In 2016, ports in developing Asia and Oceania handled 426 million TEUs of containers, thereby accounting for 61 per cent of the world port container traffic. The shares of developing economies in America (7 per cent) and Africa (4 per cent) were much smaller. Developed economies accounted for one quarter.[1]

[1] For further analyses on that topic, see UNCTAD (2017c).

Diminished growth in liner shipping **connectivity** among the world leaders

Figure 5.3.3 | **Containerized port traffic by group of economies, 2016** (Twenty-foot equivalent units)

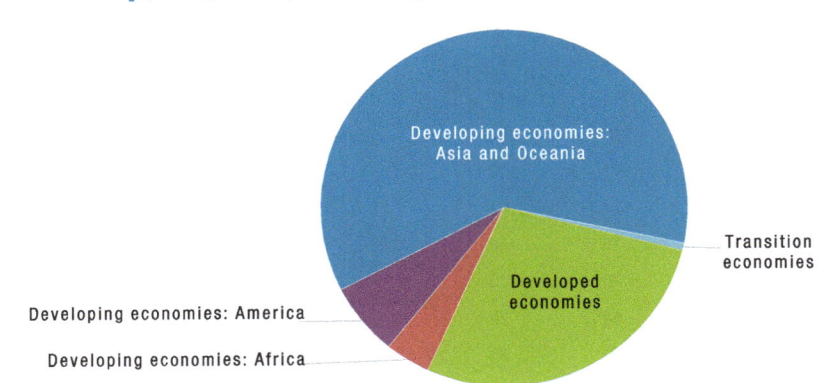

Developing economies in **Asia and Oceania** handled **61%** of world port **container traffic**

Table 5.3.1 | **Liner shipping connectivity index of most connected economies by group of economies, 2016**
(China 2004 = 100)

Developing economies: Africa

Economy (Ranked by 2016 value)	2006	2011	2015	2016
Morocco	9	55	68	60
Egypt	50	51	61	59
South Africa	26	36	41	35
Djibouti	7	21	21	33
Mauritius	12	15	30	32
Togo	11	14	20	29
Angola	9	11	20	27
Congo	9	11	20	26
Namibia	9	12	18	23
Nigeria	13	20	21	21

Developing economies: America

Economy (Ranked by 2016 value)	2006	2011	2015	2016
Panama	28	38	46	51
Colombia	20	27	42	50
Mexico	30	36	43	43
Brazil	32	35	41	39
Ecuador	14	22	22	36
Argentina	26	31	37	36
Peru	16	21	37	35
Chile	16	23	36	34
Uruguay	17	24	35	33
Bahamas	16	25	28	28

Developing economies: Asia and Oceania

Economy (Ranked by 2016 value)	2006	2011	2015	2016
China	113	152	167	171
Singapore	86	105	117	120
Korea, Republic of	72	92	113	113
Malaysia	69	91	111	102
China, Hong Kong SAR	99	115	117	101
China, Taiwan Province of	66	67	76	78
United Arab Emirates	47	63	70	73
Sri Lanka	37	41	54	62
Viet Nam	15	50	46	62
Saudi Arabia	41	60	65	61

Transition economies

Economy (Ranked by 2016 value)	2006	2011	2015	2016
Russian Federation	13	21	43	41
Ukraine	15	21	30	28
Georgia	3	4	6	13
Montenegro	–	4	3	7
Albania	0	5	4	4

Developed economies

Economy (Ranked by 2016 value)	2006	2011	2015	2016
United States	86	82	97	94
United Kingdom	82	87	95	94
Germany	81	93	98	90
Belgium	76	88	87	86
Netherlands	81	92	96	84
Spain	62	77	85	81
Japan	65	68	69	74
France	68	72	77	67
Italy	58	70	67	63
Poland	8	27	51	56

Table 5.3.2 | **Liner shipping bilateral connectivity indices of the world's seven most connected economies** (China 2004 = 100)

Economy (Ranked by LSCI 2016)	Year	LSCI	Linear shipping bilateral connectivity index vis-à-vis ...						
			China	Singapore	Korea, Rep. of	Malaysia	China, Hong Kong SAR	United States	United Kingdom
China	2011	152	–	0.787	0.784	0.757	0.847	0.685	0.720
	2016	171	–	0.816	0.852	0.817	0.801	0.734	0.756
Singapore	2011	105		–	0.704	0.794	0.751	0.607	0.665
	2016	120		–	0.779	0.845	0.741	0.682	0.719
Korea, Republic of	2011	92			–	0.619	0.760	0.633	0.584
	2016	113			–	0.773	0.703	0.700	0.732
Malaysia	2011	91				–	0.730	0.585	0.609
	2016	102				–	0.740	0.673	0.724
China, Hong Kong SAR	2011	115					–	0.678	0.707
	2016	101					–	0.701	0.684
United States	2011	82						–	0.616
	2016	94						–	0.742
United Kingdom	2011	87							–
	2016	94							–

6

Annexes

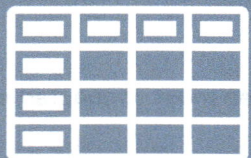

6.1 Key indicators by economy, 2016

Economy	Merchandise trade			Trade in services		GDP	
	Exports	Imports	Terms of trade	Exports	Imports	Per capita (nominal)	Growth (real)[a]
	(Millions of US$)	(Millions of US$)	(2000=100)	(Millions of US$)	(Millions of US$)	(US$)	(Percentage)
World	**15 986 095**	**16 150 393**	**109**	**4 879 300**	**4 797 410**	**10 227**	**2.2**
Developing economies	6 988 373	6 591 306	117	1 435 740	1 817 660	4 952	3.7
Developing economies: Africa	348 528	493 887	154	95 720	144 340	1 829	1.7
Developing economies: Eastern Africa	36 181	78 348	121	21 010	24 330	906	4.6
Burundi	109	616	155	(e) 73	(e) 217	263	2.0
Comoros	31	219	131	-	-	1 385	2.2
Djibouti	140	1 128	91	-	-	2 021	6.7
Eritrea	(e) 345	(e) 1 055	87	-	-	1 118	3.6
Ethiopia	2 919	(e) 16 588	141	(e) 2 981	(e) 3 627	652	5.4
Kenya	5 694	14 106	102	(e) 3 885	(e) 3 095	1 426	6.0
Madagascar	2 160	2 855	85	(e) 984	(e) 1 022	395	2.6
Malawi	1 087	2 084	119	(e) 94	(e) 245	308	2.4
Mauritius	2 359	4 655	91	(e) 2 867	(e) 2 068	9 415	3.6
Mozambique	3 355	5 295	90	(e) 422	(e) 3 203	407	4.2
Rwanda	(e) 744	(e) 2 293	178	851	1 062	699	6.7
Seychelles	(e) 448	(e) 1 043	76	(e) 894	(e) 507	14 818	3.5
Somalia	(e) 440	(e) 1 080	93	258	1 237	-	3.4
South Sudan	..	..	..	(e) 37	(e) 383	5 228	1.0
Uganda	2 543	(e) 5 099	122	(e) 1 606	(e) 2 271	639	5.0
United Republic of Tanzania	5 172	9 488	170	(e) 3 720	(e) 2 088	866	7.0
Zambia	(e) 5 801	(e) 7 045	169	(e) 885	(e) 1 393	1 302	3.0
Zimbabwe	2 832	(e) 3 700	109	-	-	840	-0.8
Developing economies: Middle Africa	52 747	38 492	131	4 410	25 760	1 479	1.8
Angola	27 306	12 538	132	(e) 1 156	(e) 12 546	4 078	0.8
Cameroon	(e) 3 966	(e) 6 855	135	-	-	1 284	5.3
Central African Republic	(e) 93	(e) 382	77	-	-	392	5.1
Chad	(e) 1 600	(e) 2 200	114	-	-	670	1.1
Congo	(e) 3 573	(e) 4 951	128	-	-	1 744	1.6
Dem. Rep. of the Congo	(e) 5 526	(e) 5 648	113	-	-	488	4.0
Equatorial Guinea	(e) 4 800	(e) 2 800	117	-	-	10 923	-4.5
Gabon	5 871	2 977	121	-	-	7 291	3.2
Sao Tome and Principe	10	139	163	88	60	1 851	5.5
Developing economies: Northern Africa	98 430	179 768	147	38 420	45 320	3 143	2.3
Algeria	28 883	46 727	84	(e) 3 561	(e) 10 822	4 088	2.9
Egypt	25 468	55 789	147	(e) 14 305	(e) 16 978	2 968	3.4
Libya	(e) 6 000	(e) 10 600	129	-	-	5 324	-4.8
Morocco	22 773	41 528	119	15 379	8 604	2 928	1.7
Sudan	(e) 1 735	5 662	-	(e) 1 585	(e) 1 523	2 343	1.0
Tunisia	13 572	19 462	114	(e) 3 136	(e) 3 002	3 490	2.0
Western Sahara	..	..	..	..	..	..	..

| Current account balance | FDI | | CPI growth | Population | | | Fleet size[b] | Economy |
| | Outflows | Inflows | | Total | Share of urban | Old-age dependency ratio | | |
(Millions of US$)	(Millions of US$)	(Millions of US$)	(Percentage)	(Millions)	(Percentage)	(Percentage)	(1000 of DWT)	
276 769	1 452 463	1 746 423	3.4	7 467	54.4	13.0	1 861 851	World
168 958	383 429	646 030	8.5	6 109	49.5	10.0	1 419 556	Developing economies
-129 136	18 173	59 373	11.8	1 224	40.9	6.3	235 656	Developing economies: Africa
-25 977	-	11 701	22.5	410	26.1	5.6	2 666	Developing economies: Eastern Africa
-536	0	0	5.5	11	12.4	4.8	..	Burundi
-58	..	8	0.1	1	28.4	5.1	885	Comoros
-542	..	160	2.7	1	77.4	6.5	62	Djibouti
(e) -233	..	52	11.8	5	23.1	6.7	14	Eritrea
-8 269	..	3 196	7.3	102	19.9	6.3	336	Ethiopia
-3 822	66	394	6.3	48	26.1	4.7	9	Kenya
-38	1	541	6.7	25	35.7	5.2	11	Madagascar
-849	-4	326	21.7	18	16.5	5.7	..	Malawi
-532	5	349	1.0	1	39.5	14.8	124	Mauritius
-4 191	..	3 093	19.9	29	32.5	6.1	27	Mozambique
-1 211	..	410	5.7	12	29.8	5.1	..	Rwanda
-286	8	155	-1.0	0	54.2	12.0	208	Seychelles
..	..	339	..	14	40.0	5.3	5	Somalia
..	..	-17	380.8	12	19.0	6.3	..	South Sudan
-1 188	..	541	5.5	41	16.4	4.4	40	Uganda
-2 009	..	1 365	5.2	56	32.3	6.0	946	United Republic of Tanzania
-929	37	469	17.9	17	41.4	4.8	0	Zambia
-	33	319	-1.6	16	32.3	5.0	..	Zimbabwe
-12 131	10 824	19 073	15.7	159	44.5	5.7	1 302	Developing economies: Middle Africa
-4 166	10 693	14 364	34.7	29	44.8	4.6	318	Angola
-1 052	10	128	0.9	23	54.9	5.9	433	Cameroon
-159	..	31	5.2	5	40.3	6.9	..	Central African Republic
-925	..	560	-4.0	14	22.6	4.9	..	Chad
-1 946	16	2 006	3.9	5	65.8	6.2	100	Congo
-1 508	272	1 205	7.3	79	43.0	6.0	71	Dem. Rep. of the Congo
(e) -1 035	..	54	1.4	1	40.1	4.8	34	Equatorial Guinea
-1 279	-168	703	2.1	2	87.4	7.5	331	Gabon
-61	1	22	5.4	0	65.6	5.5	14	Sao Tome and Principe
-72 368	1 276	14 489	9.0	229	51.5	8.6	4 955	Developing economies: Northern Africa
-26 313	55	1 546	6.4	41	71.3	9.3	652	Algeria
-20 130	207	8 107	13.8	96	43.2	8.3	1 561	Egypt
-13 491	341	493	25.0	6	78.8	6.5	2 125	Libya
-4 531	639	2 322	1.6	35	60.7	10.0	153	Morocco
-4 127	..	1 064	17.6	40	34.0	6.3	18	Sudan
-3 776	34	958	3.7	11	67.0	11.4	447	Tunisia
..	..	..	..	1	81.0	3.9	..	Western Sahara

Economy	Merchandise trade			Trade in services		GDP	
	Exports	Imports	Terms of trade	Exports	Imports	Per capita (nominal)	Growth (real)[a]
	(Millions of US$)	(Millions of US$)	(2000=100)	(Millions of US$)	(Millions of US$)	(US$)	(Percentage)
Developing economies: Southern Africa	88 903	107 697	126	16 500	17 010	5 029	0.8
Botswana	7 362	6 138	91	(e) 1 299	-	6 537	2.8
Lesotho	894	1 851	85	(e) 36	(e) 277	861	2.2
Namibia	3 979	6 721	129	(e) 660	(e) 809	4 397	2.5
South Africa	75 091	(e) 91 580	128	14 360	14 954	5 210	0.6
Swaziland	1 578	1 406	118	(e) 143	(e) 326	2 925	1.6
Developing economies: Western Africa	72 266	89 582	167	15 380	31 920	1 627	0.4
Benin	1 354	2 251	118	(e) 382	(e) 712	803	4.2
Burkina Faso	2 400	3 171	145	(e) 425	(e) 1 241	618	4.6
Cabo Verde	60	666	113	590	353	3 003	3.0
Côte d'Ivoire	11 793	10 050	174	(e) 783	(e) 3 069	1 469	8.0
Gambia	107	368	104	-	-	502	2.1
Ghana	(e) 11 283	(e) 13 352	167	(e) 6 088	(e) 6 298	1 525	3.8
Guinea	2 414	(e) 2 151	101	-	-	678	4.7
Guinea-Bissau	263	249	99	(e) 37	(e) 135	567	3.9
Liberia	170	1 311	121	(e) 183	(e) 656	495	2.3
Mali	2 538	3 509	171	(e) 435	(e) 2 419	745	4.5
Mauritania	1 399	1 951	140	(e) 181	(e) 670	1 175	4.3
Niger	1 053	2 088	156	(e) 252	(e) 1 035	359	4.1
Nigeria	32 800	39 000	129	(e) 3 718	(e) 12 318	2 303	-1.6
Saint Helena	65	40	70	..	..	..	..
Senegal	2 640	5 478	112	(e) 1 230	(e) 1 374	946	6.3
Sierra Leone	635	1 560	48	-	-	532	4.7
Togo	1 293	2 387	129	(e) 530	(e) 397	570	5.5
Developing economies: America	885 924	931 533	127	171 120	202 740	9 256	-0.5
Developing economies: Caribbean	25 065	56 564	128	37 490	17 170	6 180	2.0
Anguilla	7	193	115	(e) 142	(e) 69	22 083	2.5
Antigua and Barbuda	78	503	58	(e) 540	(e) 238	13 923	4.2
Aruba	(e) 300	(e) 1 208	100	(e) 2 040	(e) 867	25 416	-0.5
Bahamas	444	2 594	80	(e) 2 822	(e) 1 640	22 552	0.0
Barbados	517	1 622	123	(e) 1 513	(e) 743	15 804	1.4
Bonaire, Sint Eustatius and Saba	1	80	..	..	..	..	..
British Virgin Islands	(e) 23	(e) 210	55	-	-	30 872	2.2
Cayman Islands	(e) 34	(e) 925	66	-	-	62 491	2.1
Cuba	(e) 2 900	(e) 10 350	180	(e) 11 242	(e) 2 081	7 969	0.4
Curaçao	416	1 422	-	(e) 1 521	(e) 902	(u) 19 832	0.3
Dominica	23	214	117	(e) 152	(e) 98	7 054	1.0
Dominican Republic	9 860	17 484	103	(e) 8 311	(e) 3 310	6 661	6.4
Grenada	30	351	98	(e) 196	(e) 110	9 305	2.9
Haiti	995	3 423	62	(e) 608	(e) 1 006	729	2.0
Jamaica	1 202	4 767	86	(e) 3 221	(e) 2 129	4 785	1.1
Montserrat	4	36	96	(e) 15	(e) 17	11 695	2.0
Saint Kitts and Nevis	51	332	72	(e) 301	(e) 166	16 465	3.7
Saint Lucia	120	654	115	(e) 466	(e) 190	8 116	2.8

Current account balance	FDI		CPI growth	Population			Fleet size[b]	Economy
	Outflows	Inflows		Total	Share of urban	Old-age dependency ratio		
(Millions of US$)	(Millions of US$)	(Millions of US$)	(Percentage)	(Millions)	(Percentage)	(Percentage)	(1000 of DWT)	
-8 112	3 971	2 677	6.2	64	62.1	7.7	448	Developing economies: Southern Africa
2 941	583	10	3.8	2	57.7	5.9	..	Botswana
-190	..	132	6.6	2	27.8	7.5	..	Lesotho
-1 189	5	275	6.7	2	47.6	5.9	27	Namibia
-9 479	3 382	2 270	6.3	56	65.3	7.9	421	South Africa
-195	1	-11	7.8	1	21.3	5.3	..	Swaziland
-10 548	1 955	11 433	12.6	362	45.7	5.3	226 284	Developing economies: Western Africa
-615	17	161	-0.9	11	44.4	6.0	0	Benin
(e) -825	6	309	-0.2	19	30.7	4.6	..	Burkina Faso
-64	-9	119	-1.6	1	66.2	6.8	32	Cabo Verde
-774	9	481	0.7	24	54.9	5.3	10	Côte d'Ivoire
-96	9	-2	7.2	2	60.2	4.5	3	Gambia
-2 784	15	3 485	17.5	28	54.7	5.8	33	Ghana
-2 745	1	104	8.1	12	37.7	5.7	..	Guinea
31	2	20	1.7	2	50.1	5.3	1	Guinea-Bissau
..	41	453	8.8	5	50.1	5.5	219 397	Liberia
(e) -998	20	126	-1.8	18	40.7	5.1	..	Mali
-707	19	272	1.5	4	60.4	5.5	14	Mauritania
-1 154	31	293	0.2	21	19.0	5.4	10	Niger
2 619	1 305	4 449	15.7	186	48.6	5.2	3 639	Nigeria
..	..	..	(u) 0.0	0	39.5	..	..	Saint Helena
(e) -1 187	38	393	0.8	15	44.1	5.6	9	Senegal
-767	..	516	10.9	7	40.3	4.6	1 586	Sierra Leone
(e) -482	452	255	0.9	8	40.5	5.1	1 549	Togo
-96 803	751	142 072	28.0	634	80.0	11.6	462 432	Developing economies: America
-4 042	-70	3 307	2.9	39	68.1	13.6	104 300	Developing economies: Caribbean
-76	..	48	-0.5	0	100.0	..	0	Anguilla
-75	..	140	-0.5	0	23.4	9.7	10 153	Antigua and Barbuda
(e) 168	0	21	-0.9	0	41.3	18.2	..	Aruba
-1 106	359	522	-0.3	0	83.0	12.2	79 842	Bahamas
-206	-11	228	1.3	0	31.4	22.0	1 388	Barbados
..	..	..	..	0	74.8	..	..	Bonaire, Sint Eustatius and Saba
..	94 820	59 097	2.0	0	46.5	..	2	British Virgin Islands
..	25 736	44 968	-0.2	0	100.0	..	5 549	Cayman Islands
-	..	..	4.5	11	77.2	20.6	28	Cuba
-566	38	130	(u) 0.0	0	89.2	24.4	1 704	Curaçao
-60	..	31	0.2	0	69.8	..	693	Dominica
-978	116	2 407	1.6	11	79.8	10.7	2	Dominican Republic
-203	..	63	1.7	0	35.6	10.9	1	Grenada
-72	..	104	13.8	11	59.8	7.6	1	Haiti
-131	286	856	2.3	3	55.0	14.1	211	Jamaica
-10	..	4	-0.2	0	9.0	..	..	Montserrat
-143	..	66	-0.7	0	32.2	..	1 426	Saint Kitts and Nevis
-16	..	95	-3.1	0	18.5	13.4	..	Saint Lucia

Economy	Merchandise trade			Trade in services		GDP	
	Exports	Imports	Terms of trade	Exports	Imports	Per capita (nominal)	Growth (real)[a]
	(Millions of US$)	(Millions of US$)	(2000=100)	(Millions of US$)	(Millions of US$)	(US$)	(Percentage)
Saint Vincent and the Grenadines	47	335	102	(e) 161	(e) 94	6 859	2.1
Sint Maarten (Dutch part)	132	856	..	(e) 1 070	(e) 288	(u) 27 814	0.5
Trinidad and Tobago	7 845	(e) 8 800	122	-	-	17 891	-4.5
Turks and Caicos Islands	36	205	74	..	..	26 091	4.4
Developing economies: Central America	422 516	476 789	107	54 750	47 380	7 182	2.2
Belize	460	969	110	(e) 545	(e) 218	4 606	-2.4
Costa Rica	9 634	15 121	64	8 288	3 207	11 143	4.2
El Salvador	5 335	9 855	62	2 477	1 721	4 189	2.2
Guatemala	10 465	16 997	106	(e) 2 694	(e) 2 996	4 181	3.3
Honduras	7 841	10 559	74	(e) 2 739	(e) 1 787	2 283	3.5
Mexico	373 939	397 516	99	24 097	31 926	7 965	2.0
Nicaragua	4 782	7 062	108	(e) 1 578	(e) 1 082	2 132	4.8
Panama	(e) 10 060	(e) 18 710	258	(e) 12 329	(e) 4 446	13 696	5.2
Developing economies: South America	438 343	398 180	142	78 890	138 190	10 405	-2.3
Argentina	57 733	55 609	156	(e) 12 697	(e) 19 679	12 502	-2.0
Bolivia (Plurinational State of)	7 000	8 479	86	(e) 1 204	(e) 2 784	3 266	4.0
Brazil	185 280	143 474	112	(e) 33 300	(e) 63 750	8 532	-3.6
Chile	60 597	58 829	192	(e) 9 625	(e) 13 075	13 699	1.6
Colombia	31 394	44 890	110	7 796	10 816	5 911	2.0
Ecuador	16 798	16 324	117	(e) 2 109	(e) 3 232	6 095	-2.0
Falkland Islands (Malvinas)	(e) 250	(e) 180	103	-	-	..	..
Guyana	1 441	1 447	129	-	-	4 387	2.6
Paraguay	8 494	9 753	106	(e) 965	(e) 1 093	4 095	4.0
Peru	37 020	36 261	155	(e) 6 304	(e) 7 956	6 085	3.9
Suriname	1 447	1 247	137	165	565	6 677	-10.4
Uruguay	7 023	8 137	112	(e) 3 006	(e) 2 283	15 507	0.6
Venezuela (Bolivarian Rep. of)	23 867	13 550	160	-	-	34 917	-9.7
Developing economies: Asia	5 743 366	5 154 343	109	1 165 290	1 466 900	5 211	5.0
Developing economies: Eastern Asia	3 400 607	2 789 154	86	474 410	696 340	9 046	5.4
China	2 097 632	1 587 925	94	208 488	453 014	8 110	6.7
China, Hong Kong SAR	516 734	547 336	106	(e) 98 432	(e) 74 461	43 902	1.4
China, Macao SAR	1 257	8 925	89	(e) 32 419	(e) 4 077	74 427	-3.5
China, Taiwan Province of	280 321	230 568	70	41 443	52 407	22 445	0.9
Korea, Dem. People's Rep. of	(e) 4 320	(e) 4 850	66	-	-	-	1.4
Korea, Republic of	495 426	406 192	60	92 828	110 436	27 425	2.7
Mongolia	4 917	3 358	159	(e) 801	(e) 1 944	3 595	0.0
Developing economies: Southern Asia	401 192	529 472	142	192 450	174 700	1 805	6.7
Afghanistan	596	6 534	161	(e) 431	(e) 1 182	546	1.5
Bangladesh	34 971	44 832	68	(e) 3 585	(e) 8 519	1 338	7.0
Bhutan	525	1 002	114	144	197	2 757	6.4
India	264 402	359 774	113	(e) 161 845	(e) 133 710	1 718	7.3
Iran (Islamic Republic of)	69 000	40 000	199	(e) 10 202	(e) 14 694	5 276	4.3
Maldives	256	2 125	118	(e) 2 873	(e) 998	8 401	4.1
Nepal	696	8 649	85	(e) 1 282	(e) 1 250	755	2.2

| Current account balance | FDI | | CPI growth | Population | | | Fleet size[b] | Economy |
	Outflows	Inflows		Total	Share of urban	Old-age dependency ratio		
(Millions of US$)	(Millions of US$)	(Millions of US$)	(Percentage)	(Millions)	(Percentage)	(Percentage)	(1000 of DWT)	
-156	..	104	-0.1	0	50.9	11.0	3 280	Saint Vincent and the Grenadines
-26	3	63	(u) 0.0	0	100.0	..	..	Sint Maarten (Dutch part)
-2 395	-472	-60	3.1	1	8.4	14.0	18	Trinidad and Tobago
..	..	..	1.1	0	92.5		0	Turks and Caicos Islands
-29 281	-218	38 187	2.7	175	74.1	9.8	348 859	Developing economies: Central America
-163	2	33	0.6	0	43.8	5.9	2 968	Belize
-2 046	78	2 762	0.0	5	77.7	13.3	2	Costa Rica
-531	0	373	0.6	6	67.2	12.6	..	El Salvador
909	111	1 181	4.4	17	52.0	7.7	1	Guatemala
-799	201	1 002	2.7	9	55.3	7.2	460	Honduras
-22 420	-787	26 739	2.8	128	79.5	10.0	2 028	Mexico
-1 133	28	888	3.5	6	59.1	8.0	3	Nicaragua
-3 098	149	5 209	0.7	4	66.9	12.0	343 398	Panama
-63 480	1 039	100 579	44.0	420	83.6	12.1	9 273	Developing economies: South America
-14 901	887	5 745	41.4	44	91.9	17.3	543	Argentina
-1 928	15	410	3.6	11	68.9	10.7	157	Bolivia (Plurinational State of)
-23 530	-12 434	58 680	8.7	208	85.9	11.8	4 521	Brazil
-3 574	6 165	11 266	3.8	18	89.7	15.6	1 156	Chile
-12 236	4 516	13 593	7.5	49	76.7	10.7	107	Colombia
1 414	201	744	1.7	16	64.0	10.7	418	Ecuador
..	..	..	..	0	76.7	..	6	Falkland Islands (Malvinas)
120	26	58	0.7	1	28.7	7.9	41	Guyana
460		274	4.1	7	59.9	9.7	75	Paraguay
-5 303	303	6 863	3.6	32	78.9	10.7	514	Peru
-94		222	55.5	1	66.0	10.2	7	Suriname
-36	-4	953	9.6	3	95.5	22.7	53	Uruguay
-3 870	1 363	1 772	422.2	32	89.0	9.8	1 674	Venezuela (Bolivarian Rep. of)
390 544	363 058	442 665	2.9	4 239	47.4	10.7	496 342	Developing economies: Asia
381 465	291 243	260 033	1.8	1 514	58.3	14.2	273 630	Developing economies: Eastern Asia
196 380	183 100	133 700	2.0	1 404	56.8	14.0	78 400	China
14 886	62 460	108 126	2.4	7	100.0	21.6	173 318	China, Hong Kong SAR
	556	3 027	2.4	1	100.0	11.8	2	China, Macao SAR
72 221	17 843	8 333	1.4	24	77.3	17.4	4 485	China, Taiwan Province of
..	..	93	..	25	61.0	13.9	898	Korea, Dem. People's Rep. of
98 677	27 274	10 827	1.0	51	82.6	18.4	15 171	Korea, Republic of
-700	9	-4 072	0.6	3	72.8	5.9	1 355	Mongolia
-1 514	5 553	53 735	5.3	1 846	35.2	8.5	26 766	Developing economies: Southern Asia
-3 781	-1	100	2.2	35	27.1	4.7	..	Afghanistan
1 279	41	2 333	5.5	163	35.0	7.7	1 764	Bangladesh
-620	..	-12	4.4	1	39.4	7.0	..	Bhutan
-12 114	5 120	44 486	4.9	1 324	33.1	8.8	17 254	India
23 566	104	3 372	8.6	80	73.9	7.3	6 583	Iran (Islamic Republic of)
-840	..	448	0.5	0	46.5	5.7	74	Maldives
-168	..	106	8.8	29	19.0	9.0	..	Nepal

Economy	Merchandise trade			Trade in services		GDP	
	Exports	Imports	Terms of trade	Exports	Imports	Per capita (nominal)	Growth (real)[a]
	(Millions of US$)	(Millions of US$)	(2000=100)	(Millions of US$)	(Millions of US$)	(US$)	(Percentage)
Pakistan	20 435	47 155	63	(e) 4 949	(e) 7 953	1 478	5.3
Sri Lanka	10 310	19 400	113	(e) 7 138	(e) 6 199	4 029	4.9
Developing economies: South-Eastern Asia	1 151 851	1 086 480	97	327 300	319 820	3 986	4.5
Brunei Darussalam	5 224	2 671	104	(e) 482	(e) 2 183	30 308	0.4
Cambodia	10 069	12 632	77	(e) 4 035	(e) 1 972	1 263	6.8
Indonesia	144 840	135 653	125	24 151	30 637	3 614	5.1
Lao People's Dem. Rep.	3 352	4 739	98	-	-	2 031	7.0
Malaysia		168 392	89	(e) 33 925	(e) 39 347	9 536	4.4
Myanmar	(e) 11 240	(e) 15 380	88	-	-	1 292	8.3
Philippines	57 406	85 909	68	31 357	24 233	2 934	6.3
Singapore	338 082	291 908	86	149 642	155 581	52 479	1.8
Thailand	215 418	194 185	102	(e) 66 419	(e) 42 199	5 751	3.1
Timor-Leste	20	(e) 780	..	77	607	2 282	2.0
Viet Nam	176 785	174 231	..	(e) 12 385	(e) 18 529	2 173	6.1
Developing economies: Western Asia	789 716	749 237	180	171 130	276 030	10 564	1.9
Bahrain	12 070	8 700	118	(e) 3 170	(e) 1 742	22 900	2.0
Iraq	43 890	38 713	74	(e) 4 835	(e) 10 037	4 482	2.4
Jordan	7 509	19 207	88	(e) 6 233	(e) 4 438	4 031	2.4
Kuwait	46 273	30 825	101	5 527	26 239	29 582	2.3
Lebanon	3 930	18 955	111	-	-	8 380	1.2
Oman	24 455	23 260	106	-	-	16 243	1.8
Qatar	57 254	32 058	447	15 176	31 541	67 690	2.7
Saudi Arabia	182 304	135 891	137	15 958	71 159	21 329	1.8
State of Palestine	798	6 742	88	(e) 878	(e) 1 045	2 762	4.6
Syrian Arab Republic	1 800	4 500	151	-	-	1 185	-6.5
Turkey	142 533	198 617	103	37 634	22 215	8 939	2.0
United Arab Emirates	265 900	225 000	290	63 417	83 213	41 405	2.0
Yemen	1 000	6 770	127	-	-	1 160	-4.0
Developing economies: Oceania	10 556	11 544	153	-	-	4 004	2.3
American Samoa	(e) 390	(e) 280	170	-	-	..	..
Cook Islands	(e) 16	(e) 116		-	-	-	3.0
Fiji	926	2 316	113	(e) 1 247	(e) 469	5 147	1.5
French Polynesia	134	1 491	92	-	-	(u) 18 644	2.0
Guam	33	(e) 590	101	-	-		..
Kiribati	(e) 11	(e) 85	115	-	-	-	2.5
Marshall Islands	(e) 47	(e) 145	108	-	-	-	1.5
Micronesia (Federated States of)	(e) 75	(e) 170	109	-	-	-	1.0
Nauru	(e) 20	(e) 51	144	-	-	-	4.0
New Caledonia	1 330	2 395	158	-	-	33 699	2.5
Niue	(e) 0	(e) 11	74	-	-	..	..
Northern Mariana Islands	(e) 4	(e) 135	84	-	-	..	..
Palau	7	154	108	-	-	-	2.0
Papua New Guinea	7 020	2 050	160	(e) 106	(e) 781	2 550	2.5
Samoa	56	350	86	(e) 160	(e) 83	4 113	2.5

| Current account balance | FDI | | CPI growth | Population | | | Fleet size[b] | Economy |
| | Outflows | Inflows | | Total | Share of urban | Old-age dependency ratio | | |
(Millions of US$)	(Millions of US$)	(Millions of US$)	(Percentage)	(Millions)	(Percentage)	(Percentage)	(1000 of DWT)	
-6 895	52	2 006	3.8	193	39.2	7.4	710	Pakistan
-1 942	237	898	4.0	21	18.4	14.7	382	Sri Lanka
99 245	35 418	101 099	2.0	642	48.3	9.0	175 701	Developing economies: South-Eastern Asia
1 766	-60	-150	-0.7	0	77.5	6.0	550	Brunei Darussalam
-1 776	121	1 916	3.0	16	20.9	6.6	930	Cambodia
-16 909	-12 463	2 658	3.5	261	54.5	7.7	20 144	Indonesia
-1 234	2	890	1.5	7	39.7	6.3	2	Lao People's Dem. Rep.
6 921	5 601	9 926	2.1	31	75.4	8.8	10 059	Malaysia
-2 012		2 190	7.0	53	34.6	8.2	278	Myanmar
601	3 698	7 912	1.8	103	44.3	7.4	6 135	Philippines
56 501	23 888	61 597	-0.5	6	100.0	17.0	124 238	Singapore
47 685	13 229	1 554	0.2	69	51.5	15.3	5 375	Thailand
-533	13	5	-1.2	1	33.4	6.7		Timor-Leste
8 235	1 388	12 600	3.2	95	34.2	9.9	7 991	Viet Nam
-88 652	30 844	27 797	4.9	237	70.9	7.4	20 245	Developing economies: Western Asia
-1 493	170	282	2.8	1	88.8	3.0	426	Bahrain
..	304	-5 911	0.4	37	69.6	5.5	106	Iraq
-3 606	3	1 539	-0.8	9	83.9	6.3	105	Jordan
641	-6 258	275	3.2	4	98.4	2.9	5 155	Kuwait
-9 797	773	2 564	-0.8	6	87.9	12.2	188	Lebanon
-9 783	862	142	1.1	4	78.1	3.1	14	Oman
-8 324	7 902	774	2.9	3	99.3	1.4	1 076	Qatar
-27 551	8 359	7 453	3.5	32	83.3	4.4	3 703	Saudi Arabia
-1 348	114	269	-0.2	5	75.5	5.3	..	State of Palestine
-2 077	..	..	43.9	18	58.1	7.1	60	Syrian Arab Republic
-32 564	2 869	11 987	7.8	80	73.9	11.9	8 201	Turkey
8 782	15 711	8 986	1.6	9	85.8	1.3	771	United Arab Emirates
-1 532	35	-561	12.3	28	35.2	5.1	441	Yemen
4 353	-	1 921	3.3	11	22.7	7.1	225 126	Developing economies: Oceania
..	..	..	..	0	87.1	..	..	American Samoa
..	1 360	16	..	0	74.8	..	2 959	Cook Islands
-139	-23	270	3.9	1	54.1	9.2	218	Fiji
-	34	53	(u) 0.0	0	55.8	10.9	13	French Polynesia
..	..	..	(u) 0.0	0	94.6	14.0	0	Guam
36	3	3	..	0	44.4	6.2	510	Kiribati
..	..	21	..	0	72.9	..	216 616	Marshall Islands
..	..	..	..	0	22.5	7.4	249	Micronesia (Federated States of)
..	..	..	..	0	100.0	..	..	Nauru
-	55	1 498	0.6	0	70.7	14.6	4	New Caledonia
..	..	..	..	0	43.3	..	..	Niue
..	..	..	..	0	89.2	..	..	Northern Mariana Islands
..	..	31	..	0	87.6	..	..	Palau
(e) 6 033	0	-40	6.8	8	13.0	6.2	179	Papua New Guinea
-48	15	2	1.3	0	19.0	9.5	4	Samoa

Economy	Merchandise trade			Trade in services		GDP	
	Exports	Imports	Terms of trade	Exports	Imports	Per capita (nominal)	Growth (real)[a]
	(Millions of US$)	(Millions of US$)	(2000=100)	(Millions of US$)	(Millions of US$)	(US$)	(Percentage)
Solomon Islands	(e) 415	(e) 430	92	(e) 111	(e) 234	1 885	3.0
Tokelau	0	0	133	..	..	..	..
Tonga	(e) 22	(e) 260	112	(e) 75	(e) 87	3 754	2.5
Tuvalu	(e) 0	(e) 28	-	(e) 4	(e) 19	(u) 3 018	1.5
Vanuatu	50	422	103	(e) 334	(e) 156	2 897	4.2
Wallis and Futuna Islands	0	65	122	..	..	..	..
Transition economies	**448 106**	**376 192**	**118**	**106 920**	**126 460**	**6 113**	**0.1**
Albania	1 962	4 669	93	2 651	1 771	4 183	3.2
Armenia	1 792	3 274	123	1 610	1 734	3 624	2.5
Azerbaijan	13 211	9 004	100	(e) 4 375	(e) 7 527	3 828	-2.9
Belarus	23 416	27 570	93	6 813	4 247	8 463	-2.7
Bosnia and Herzegovina	5 267	9 126	104	1 702	485	4 647	2.1
Georgia	2 114	7 294	143	(e) 3 367	(e) 1 757	3 581	2.8
Kazakhstan	36 775	25 377	135	(e) 6 255	(e) 10 997	7 520	0.3
Kyrgyzstan	1 503	3 963	122	(e) 864	(e) 977	1 024	0.2
Montenegro	361	2 286	..	1 396	530	6 565	3.2
Republic of Moldova	2 045	4 021	73	1 047	835	1 622	1.2
Russian Federation	281 681	191 672	133	50 504	74 379	8 916	-0.5
Serbia	14 852	19 231	109	(e) 6 220	(e) 4 607	5 024	2.8
Tajikistan	977	4 297	89	232	369	813	6.4
TFYR of Macedonia	4 787	6 757	97	1 598	1 156	4 912	2.3
Turkmenistan	(e) 11 000	(e) 7 000	122	-	-	7 759	6.0
Ukraine	36 364	39 151	83	(e) 12 394	(e) 11 185	2 001	0.8
Uzbekistan	(e) 10 000	(e) 11 500	158			2 271	7.4
Developed economies	**8 549 616**	**9 182 895**	**102**	**3 336 640**	**2 853 290**	**42 063**	**1.6**
Developed economies: America	**1 845 512**	**2 669 640**	**104**	**834 660**	**601 500**	**55 768**	**1.6**
Bermuda	(e) 18	975	103	(e) 1 319	(e) 1 065	97 153	0.9
Canada	390 331	416 602	106	(e) 80 927	(e) 97 378	42 387	1.2
Greenland	552	623	93	-	-	(u) 37 544	2.0
Saint Pierre and Miquelon	3	89	108	-	-	..	..
United States	1 454 607	2 251 351	100	(e) 752 411	(e) 503 053	57 253	1.6
Developed economies: Asia	**705 060**	**676 438**	**96**	**212 720**	**208 490**	**38 469**	**1.1**
Israel	60 160	68 835	113	(e) 38 899	(e) 23 782	37 819	2.8
Japan	644 900	607 602	95	173 821	184 710	38 511	1.0
Developed economies: Europe	**5 774 152**	**5 604 617**	**99**	**2 220 430**	**1 974 810**	**33 069**	**1.8**
Andorra	(e) 84	1 355	104	..	..	(u) 36 286	0.0
Austria	152 209	157 618	90	(e) 60 020	(e) 48 772	44 150	1.4
Belgium	397 977	372 603	95	(e) 111 017	(e) 107 417	41 321	1.4
Bulgaria	25 965	28 838	131	(e) 8 452	(e) 4 530	6 993	2.9
Croatia	13 816	21 876	73	(e) 13 490	(e) 3 906	11 813	2.6
Cyprus	2 962	7 817	55	(e) 9 830	(e) 5 542	22 965	1.6
Czechia	162 796	142 823	105	(e) 23 759	(e) 19 777	18 170	2.8
Denmark	95 387	85 695	101	(e) 58 691	(e) 55 384	53 699	1.6
Estonia	13 171	14 935	88	(e) 6 108	(e) 4 191	17 350	1.5

Current account balance	FDI		CPI growth	Population			Fleet size[b]	Economy
	Outflows	Inflows		Total	Share of urban	Old-age dependency ratio		
(Millions of US$)	(Millions of US$)	(Millions of US$)	(Percentage)	(Millions)	(Percentage)	(Percentage)	(1000 of DWT)	
-49	1	25	2.5	1	22.8	6.1	4	Solomon Islands
..	..	..	..	0	0.0	..	..	Tokelau
(e) -66	1	9	2.6	0	23.8	10.1	73	Tonga
-2	..	0	(u) 0.0	0	60.6	..	1 986	Tuvalu
-93	1	32	0.9	0	26.4	7.2	2 311	Vanuatu
..	..	..	..	0	0.0	..	..	Wallis and Futuna Islands
-5 413	25 096	67 772	8.0	306	63.4	17.5	10 672	Transition economies
-1 142	64	1 124	1.3	3	58.4	18.5	54	Albania
-238	57	338	-1.3	3	62.6	16.0	..	Armenia
-1 363	2 574	4 500	12.6	10	54.9	8.2	738	Azerbaijan
-1 703	28	1 235	11.8	9	77.0	21.1	1	Belarus
-741	12	285	-1.3	4	39.9	23.2	..	Bosnia and Herzegovina
-1 935	232	1 661	2.1	4	53.8	22.2	82	Georgia
-8 518	-5 367	9 069	14.5	18	53.2	10.4	161	Kazakhstan
-663	0	467	0.4	6	35.9	6.8	..	Kyrgyzstan
-788	-185	226	-0.3	1	64.2	21.2	140	Montenegro
-277	-9	143	6.4	4	45.1	14.0	714	Republic of Moldova
25 543	27 272	37 668	7.1	144	74.1	20.0	8 277	Russian Federation
-1 513	240	2 299	1.1	9	55.7	25.3	..	Serbia
-265	..	434	8.0	9	26.9	5.5	..	Tajikistan
-341	5	397	-0.2	2	57.2	18.3	..	TFYR of Macedonia
-7 605	..	4 522	11.0	6	50.4	6.4	121	Turkmenistan
-3 779	173	3 336	13.9	44	69.9	23.6	384	Ukraine
(e) -84		67	12.0	31	36.5	6.4		Uzbekistan
113 225	1 043 884	1 032 373	0.7	1 052	80.3	28.7	427 235	Developed economies
-501 556	365 497	425 185	1.3	362	81.9	23.0	25 750	Developed economies: America
766	91	360	1.4	0	100.0	..	10 958	Bermuda
-50 630	66 403	33 721	1.4	36	82.0	24.6	2 992	Canada
..	..	..	(u) 0.0	0	86.8	..	2	Greenland
..	..	..	..	0	90.5	..	..	Saint Pierre and Miquelon
-451 692	299 003	391 104	1.3	326	81.9	22.8	11 798	United States
198 415	157 743	23 712	-0.1	136	93.8	42.4	34 848	Developed economies: Asia
11 150	12 501	12 324	-0.5	8	92.2	18.9	319	Israel
187 265	145 242	11 388	-0.1	128	93.9	43.9	34 529	Japan
453 999	514 677	532 994	0.4	525	75.1	29.7	364 579	Developed economies: Europe
..	..	..	(u) 0.0	0	84.6	..	..	Andorra
6 618	-2 208	-6 089	0.9	9	66.0	28.5	..	Austria
-1 913	18 269	33 103	2.0	11	97.9	28.4	8 040	Belgium
2 238	190	776	-0.8	7	74.3	31.3	116	Bulgaria
1 390	-422	1 745	-1.1	4	59.3	29.3	2 073	Croatia
-1 023	5 376	4 138	-1.4	(e) 1	(e) 66.8	18.7	33 765	Cyprus
2 139	984	6 752	0.6	11	73.0	28.0	..	Czechia
24 339	14 543	951	0.3	6	87.8	30.4	16 893	Denmark
477	479	870	0.1	1	67.5	29.6	85	Estonia

Economy	Merchandise trade			Trade in services		GDP	
	Exports	Imports	Terms of trade	Exports	Imports	Per capita (nominal)	Growth (real)[a]
	(Millions of US$)	(Millions of US$)	(2000=100)	(Millions of US$)	(Millions of US$)	(US$)	(Percentage)
Faeroe Islands	1 183	976	120	-	-	..	..
Finland	57 426	60 691	93	(e) 25 439	28 369	42 570	0.9
France	500 885	572 658	91	(e) 236 760	(e) 235 679	36 619	1.1
Germany	1 337 854	1 055 087	102	(e) 272 738	(e) 312 074	41 893	1.8
Gibraltar	(e) 250	(e) 700	56	-	-	..	..
Greece	28 146	48 735	89	(e) 27 777	(e) 10 715	17 183	-0.3
Holy See	..	..	..	..	..	..	..
Hungary	101 937	93 671	102	(e) 23 079	(e) 16 307	12 681	2.0
Iceland	4 456	5 699	91	5 409	3 234	57 836	3.2
Ireland	128 909	78 788	89	(e) 146 678	(e) 191 939	62 209	3.9
Italy	461 512	404 511	106	(e) 101 402	(e) 103 990	30 807	0.9
Latvia	12 101	14 328	101	(e) 4 696	(e) 2 618	13 892	1.5
Lithuania	25 012	27 485	96	(e) 7 445	(e) 5 069	14 614	2.0
Luxembourg	15 772	21 687	73	(e) 94 579	(e) 71 763	101 259	2.6
Malta	3 015	6 209	130	(e) 11 351	(e) 8 774	23 501	3.2
Netherlands	569 430	504 309	96	(e) 179 776	(e) 169 458	45 077	2.0
Norway	89 483	72 669	115	36 404	47 092	73 646	0.7
Poland	202 515	197 279	101	(e) 49 010	(e) 33 847	12 168	2.6
Portugal	55 675	67 614	108	(e) 29 297	(e) 14 769	19 534	1.4
Romania	63 527	74 538	107	(e) 19 841	(e) 11 399	9 127	4.9
San Marino	..	..	..	..	..	47 750	1.0
Slovakia	77 618	75 487	94	(e) 8 323	(e) 7 950	16 445	3.4
Slovenia	32 885	30 489	95	(e) 7 210	(e) 4 677	21 034	2.5
Spain	288 704	310 122	92	(e) 127 132	(e) 70 960	26 439	3.2
Sweden	139 408	140 756	93	(e) 71 773	(e) 60 933	51 732	3.2
Switzerland	302 901	270 113	110	114 356	95 207	79 047	1.3
United Kingdom	409 182	636 456	98	(e) 327 176	(e) 198 653	39 263	2.0
Developed economies: Oceania	224 892	232 200	146	68 830	68 500	50 411	2.5
Australia	191 152	196 137	147	(e) 53 941	(e) 56 532	52 665	2.4
New Zealand	33 740	36 063	137	(e) 14 886	(e) 11 967	38 745	3.2
Selected groups							
Developing economies excluding China	4 890 741	5 003 381	121	1 227 250	1 364 640	4 009	2.4
Developing economies excluding LDCs	6 841 354	6 373 059	116	1 399 410	1 748 870	5 696	3.7
LDCs	147 019	218 247	145	36 330	68 780	1 061	4.0
LLDCs	141 224	175 879	135	37 480	55 870	1 489	2.7
SIDS (UNCTAD)	15 170	34 210	119	20 020	14 200	7 132	0.3
HIPCs (IMF)	100 687	159 139	137	34 700	54 820	803	4.5
BRICS	2 904 086	2 374 426	114	468 500	739 810	5 423	4.7
G20	9 691 285	9 844 308	107	2 675 040	2 717 930	13 057	2.2

[a] At constant 2005 United States dollars.
[b] As of 1 January 2017.

| Current account balance | FDI | | CPI growth | Population | | | Fleet size[b] | Economy |
| | Outflows | Inflows | | Total | Share of urban | Old-age dependency ratio | | |
(Millions of US$)	(Millions of US$)	(Millions of US$)	(Percentage)	(Millions)	(Percentage)	(Percentage)	(1000 of DWT)	
..	..	..	(u) 0.0	0	42.2	..	356	Faeroe Islands
-2 551	22 760	42	0.4	6	84.4	33.1	1 184	Finland
-22 531	57 328	28 352	0.3	67	80.0	30.6	6 967	France
288 963	34 558	9 528	0.5	82	75.5	32.4	10 444	Germany
..	..	-883	(u) 0.0	0	100.0	..	2 979	Gibraltar
-1 239	-638	3 126	-0.8	11	78.3	30.8	74 638	Greece
..	..	..	..	0	100.0	..	..	Holy See
6 753	-8 823	-5 314	0.4	10	71.7	26.6	..	Hungary
1 571	-1 199	-484	1.7	0	94.2	21.4	15	Iceland
13 871	44 548	22 304	0.0	5	63.5	21.0	284	Ireland
47 429	22 794	28 955	-0.1	59	69.1	35.7	15 944	Italy
403	178	126	0.1	2	67.4	29.9	80	Latvia
-398	-136	-208	0.9	3	66.5	28.4	165	Lithuania
2 788	31 643	26 857	0.3	1	90.4	20.4	2 248	Luxembourg
765	-5 362	3 575	0.6	0	95.5	28.4	99 216	Malta
65 711	173 658	91 956	0.3	17	91.0	28.2	7 619	Netherlands
18 384	14 876	-5 533	3.6	5	80.7	25.3	21 900	Norway
-959	6 436	11 358	-0.6	38	60.5	23.5	105	Poland
1 708	1 583	6 065	0.6	10	64.0	32.5	13 753	Portugal
-4 385	241	4 573	-1.5	20	54.7	25.9	58	Romania
..	..	..	0.6	0	94.2	..	..	San Marino
-641	248	-295	-0.5	5	53.5	20.7	..	Slovakia
2 337	98	919	-0.1	2	49.6	27.8	1	Slovenia
23 743	41 789	18 659	-0.2	46	79.8	29.0	1 810	Spain
22 908	22 851	19 584	1.0	10	86.0	31.6	1 098	Sweden
70 632	30 648	-26 340	-0.4	8	73.7	27.2	1 758	Switzerland
-115 527	-12 614	253 826	0.6	66	82.7	28.7	40 986	United Kingdom
-37 633	5 968	50 482	1.8	29	89.0	23.1	2 058	Developed economies: Oceania
-33 012	6 012	48 190	1.9	24	89.6	23.2	1 883	Australia
-4 621	-44	2 292	1.1	5	86.3	23.0	176	New Zealand
								Selected groups
-27 423	200 329	512 330	11.3	4 705	47.3	8.7	1 341 155	Developing economies excluding China
221 282	371 579	608 087	8.3	5 128	52.8	10.6	1 185 980	Developing economies excluding LDCs
-52 324	11 851	37 944	15.6	981	32.1	6.3	233 576	LDCs
-43 096	-2 009	24 326	14.8	492	29.3	6.5	3 708	LLDCs
-7 226	-169	2 296	1.5	13	40.9	11.2	320 322	SIDS (UNCTAD)
-45 625	1 262	23 328	6.1	686	35.1	5.8	226 138	HIPCs (IMF)
176 801	206 440	276 803	3.9	3 135	49.7	11.9	108 873	BRICS
11 397	851 305	1 147 276	1.9	4 519	57.9	14.6	284 204	G20

6.2 Classifications

Classification of economies

There is no established convention for the designation of "developing", "transition" and "developed" countries or areas in the United Nations system. The designation of economies used in this handbook is the classification used by UNCTAD. The differentiation between developing and developed economies follows, in general, the definition of the M49 classification (United Nations, 2017d). However, there are exceptions. Notably, the group 'Transition economies' that was established to take account of the particular circumstances of that group of economies; shaped by socialism and the transition to a market economy. The geographic locations of developing, transition and developed economies are depicted by the map titled "The world by development status" on the first pages of this handbook.

Throughout the handbook, the group of developing economies is further broken down into the following three regions: "Africa", "America", "Asia and Oceania". Furthermore, whenever possible, data are also presented for the following eight groups:

* developing economies excluding China,

* developing economies excluding LDCs,

* LDCs, according to the United Nations Office of the High Representative for the Least Developed Countries, Landlocked Developing Countries and the Small Island Developing States (UN-OHRLLS) (United Nations, 2017e),

* LLDCs, according to UN-OHRLLS (ibid.),

* SIDS according to UNCTAD (2017d),

* HIPC, according to the International Monetary Fund (2017),

* Brazil, Russia, India, China and South Africa (BRICS),

* Group of Twenty (G20) (Germany, 2017).

The UNCTADstat classification page (UNCTAD, 2017a) provides the lists of the economies included in the different groups.

Classification of goods

For breakdowns of international merchandise trade by product, UNCTADstat applies the SITC, Revision 3, (United Nations, 2017f) and various aggregates compiled on the basis of that classification. In this handbook, reference is made to the following five product groups:

* All food items (SITC divisions: 0, 1, 22, 4),

* Agricultural raw materials (SITC division 2 without 22, 27 and 28),

* Ores, metals, precious stones and non-monetary gold (SITC divisions: 27, 28, 68, 667, 971),

* Fuels (SITC division 3),

* Manufactured goods (SITC divisions: 5, 6, 7, 8 without 667 and 68).

Classification of services

The breakdowns by service category in section 2.2 are based on the Extended Balance of Payments Services (EBOPS) 2010 classification (United Nations et al., 2012). The EBOPS categories have been grouped as shown in the table below.

Table 6.2 | Grouping of service categories on the basis of EBOPS 2010

UNCTADstat	EBOPS 2010	Figures 2.2.1 and 2.2.2
Transport	Transport	Transport
Travel	Travel	Travel
Other services	Insurance and pension services	Insurance, pension, financial services
	Financial services	
	Charges for the use of intellectual property n.i.e.	Intellectual property, other business services
	Other business services	
	Telecommunications, computer and information services	Telecommunications, computer and information services
	Personal, cultural and recreational services	Other categories
	Government goods and services n.i.e.	
	Construction	
	Services not allocated	
Goods-related services	Manufacturing services on physical inputs owned by others	
	Maintenance and repair services n.i.e.	

Classification of economic activities

In section 3.1, gross value added is broken down by the three broad groups of economic activities below, in accordance with the International Standard Industrial Classification of All Economic Activities (ISIC), Revision 3 (United Nations, 2017g):

- Agriculture, comprising: agriculture, hunting, forestry and fishing (ISIC divisiona 01–05),
- Industry, comprising: mining and quarrying, manufacturing, electricity, gas and water supply, construction (ISIC divisions 10–45),
- Services, comprising all other economic activities (ISIC divisions: 50–99).

6.3 Calculation methods

The **annual average growth rate** is, unless otherwise specified, computed as the coefficient b in the exponential trend function $y = ae^{bt}$ where t stands for time and y is the object of measurement. This method takes all observations in the analysed period into account. Therefore, the growth rate reflects trends that are less influenced by exceptional values.

In chapter 4, annual population growth is expressed by the **annual exponential rate of growth**, defined as:

$$b = \ln\left(\frac{y_t}{y_{t-1}}\right)$$

The **product concentration index of exports** (map 1.4) is calculated as a normalized Herfindahl-Hirschmann index:

$$PCI_{exports,j} = \frac{\sqrt{\sum_{i=1}^{n}\left(\frac{x_{i,j}}{X_j}\right)^2} - \sqrt{\frac{1}{n}}}{1 - \sqrt{\frac{1}{n}}}, \text{ with } X_j = \sum_{i=1}^{n} x_{i,j},$$

where $x_{i,j}$ is the value of exports of product i from economy j and n is the number of product groups according to SITC, Revision 3, at the 3-digit level.

The **terms of trade index** (figure 1.4.1, tables 1.4.1 and 1.4.2) with base year 2000 is calculated as follows:

$$ToT_{i,t} = 100 \frac{\frac{UVI_{exports,i,t}}{UVI_{imports,i,t}}}{\frac{UVI_{exports,i,2000}}{UVI_{imports,i,2000}}}$$

where $UVI_{exports,i,t}$ is the unit value index of exports and $UVI_{imports,i,t}$ the unit value index of imports of economy i at time t.

The **market concentration index of exports** (figure 1.4.2) is calculated as a normalized Herfindahl-Hirschmann index:

$$MCI_{exports,i} = \frac{\sqrt{\sum_{j=1}^{n}\left(\frac{x_{i,j}}{X_i}\right)^2} - \sqrt{\frac{1}{n}}}{1 - \sqrt{\frac{1}{n}}}, \text{ with } X_i = \sum_{j=1}^{n} x_{i,j},$$

where x_{ij} is the value of exports of product i from economy j and n is the number of economies.

The **trade openness index** (figure 1.4.3) is calculated as the ratio of the arithmetic mean of merchandise exports (x) and imports (m) to GDP (y):

$$TOI_{i,t} = \frac{\frac{1}{2}(x_{i,t} + m_{i,t})}{y_{i,t}}$$

where i designates the economy and t the year.

The **volume index of exports (imports)** (tables 1.4.1 and 1.4.2) is calculated by dividing the export (import) value index by the corresponding unit value index and scaling up by 100:

$$QI_{i,t} = 100 \, \frac{VI_{i,t}}{UVI_{i,t}}$$

where $VI_{i,t}$ is the value index of exports (imports), given by

$$VI_{i,t} = 100 \, \frac{x_{i,t}}{x_{i,2000}}$$

$x_{i,t}$ is the value of exports (imports), $UVI_{i,t}$ is the unit value index of exports (imports), i designates the economy and t the time period.

The **purchasing power index of exports** (table 1.4.1) is calculated by dividing the export value index by the corresponding import unit value index and scaling up by 100:

$$PPI_{exports,i,t} = 100 \, \frac{VI_{exports,i,t}}{UVI_{imports,i,t}}$$

where $VI_{exports,i,t}$ is the value index of exports (as defined above), $UVI_{imports,i,t}$ is the unit value index of imports, i designates the economy and t the time period.

The **Lorenz curve** in figure 3.1.3 plots cumulative population shares ordered by GDP per capita, on the x-axis, against the cumulative shares of global GDP which they account for, on the y-axis. For the construction of the Lorenz curve, the n economies of the world are ordered with reference to their GDP per capita, so that

$$\frac{y_i}{p_i} \geq \frac{y_{i-1}}{p_{i-1}} \quad \text{for all } i \in \{2, 3, ..., n\}$$

where y_i is GDP and p_i the population of the economy at position i in this ranking, counted from below.

The cumulative population shares, measured on the x-axis, are calculated as

$$P_i = \sum_{j=1}^{i} \frac{p_j}{p} \quad \text{with } p = p_1 + p_2 + ... + p_n$$

The cumulative shares of global GDP, measured on the y-axis, are calculated as follows:

$$Y_i = \sum_{j=1}^{i} \frac{y_j}{y} \quad \text{with } y = y_1 + y_2 + ... + y_n$$

6.4 References

Germany (2017). G20: Members and Participants. Available at www.g20.org/Webs/G20/DE/Home/home_node.html.

International Monetary Fund (2009). *Balance of Payments and International Investment Position Manual. Sixth Edition (BPM6)*. Washington, D.C.

International Monetary Fund (2017). Debt Relief under the Heavily Indebted Poor Countries Initiative. Available at www. imf.org/en/About/Factsheets/Sheets/2016/08/01/16/11/Debt-Relief-Under-the-Heavily-Indebted-Poor-Countries-Initiative.

UNCTAD (2017a). UNCTADstat. See http://unctadstat.unctad.org.

UNCTAD (2017b). *World Investment Report 2017: Investment and the Digital Economy*. United Nations publication. Sales no. E.17.II.D.3. Geneva.

UNCTAD (2017c). *Review of Maritime Transport 2017*. United Nations publication, Sales no. E.17.II.D.10. New York and Geneva.

UNCTAD (2017d). UNCTAD's Unofficial List of SIDS. Available at http://unctad.org/en/pages/aldc/Small%20Island%20 Developing%20States/UNCTAD%C2%B4s-unofficial-list-of-SIDS.aspx.

United Nations (2011). *International Merchandise Trade Statistics: Concepts and Definitions 2010*. Department of Economic and Social Affairs, Statistics Division, Statistical Papers, ST/ESA/STAT/SER.M/52/Rev.3, New York.

United Nations (2017a). UN Comtrade Database. See https://comtrade.un.org.

United Nations (2017b). *World Population Prospects: The 2017 Revision, Key Findings and Advance Tables*. Department of Economic and Social Affairs, Population Division. Working Paper No. ESA/P/WP/248. New York.

United Nations (2017c). World Urbanization Prospects, the 2014 Revision: Glossary of Demographic Terms. Available at https://esa.un.org/unpd/wup/General/GlossaryDemographicTerms.aspx.

United Nations (2017d). Methodology: Standard Country or Area Codes for Statistical Use (M49). Available at https:// unstats.un.org/unsd/methodology/m49/.

United Nations (2017e). UN-OHRLLS. See http://unohrlls.org.

United Nations (2017f). Standard International Trade Classification, Rev.3. Available at https://unstats.un.org/unsd/cr/ registry/regcst.asp?Cl=14&Lg=.

United Nations (2017g). International Standard Industrial Classification of All Economic Activities, Rev.3. Available at https://unstats.un.org/unsd/cr/registry/regcst.asp?Cl=2&Lg=1.

United Nations, European Commission, International Monetary Fund, Organisation for Economic Co-operation and Development, World Bank (2009). *System of National Accounts 2008*, ST/ESA/STAT/SER.F/2/Rev.5, Sales No. E.08. XVII.29, New York.

United Nations, Statistical Office of the European Union, International Monetary Fund, Organisation for Economic Co-operation and Development, UNCTAD, World Tourism Organization, World Trade Organization (2012). *Manual on Statistics of International Trade in Services 2010*. ST/ESA/M.86/Rev. 1. United Nations publication, Sales No. E.10. XVII.14, Geneva.